LEWIS JOSSELYN, CARMEL PHOTOGRAPHER

GREGORY FORD HENDERSON

LEWIS JOSSELYN

Published by Kindle Direct Publishing
https://kdp.amazon.com/en_US/

ISBN: 979-8340824257

Dedicated to the photographers of Carmel-by-the-Sea.

TABLE OF CONTENTS

Preface

This story is about photographer Lewis Josselyn, an early American photographer recognized for his extensive work in landscape, theatrical, and portrait photography. As an early member of the art colony in Carmel-by-the-Sea, California, he made a lasting impact over his half-century career. Josselyn gained recognition as the official photographer for the Forest Theater, where he captured dramatic images of actors and stage sets from many productions from 1915 through the 1940s.

His portfolio also includes iconic photographs of poet Robinson Jeffers at his home, Tor House and Hawk Tower, as well as portraits of notable figures like artist Jo Mora, painter William Ritschel, and real estate developer Frank Devendorf.

As stories and photographs often fade with time, my hope is that this book will preserve Lewis Josselyn's legacy and help future generations gain a deeper understanding of his works and contributions.

Greg Henderson
December 14, 2024

Acknowledgments

I would like to thank the following individuals for their contributions to the creation of this book: James Perry, Director of the Monterey County Historical Society, for granting permission to use the Lewis Josselyn photographs; Peter Hiller, Curator of the Jo Mora Trust Collection, for his insights and expertise; Katie O'Connell, Librarian at the Harrison Memorial Library, for her generous support; Trudy Salter, daughter of Winsor Josselyn, for sharing her family's history and authorizing the use of several photographs; and Barbara Josselyn Asa and Rachel Josselyn Asa, mother and granddaughter of Talbert Josselyn, for permitting the inclusion of images of Talbert, Winsor, and Lewis Josselyn.

A special thanks goes to my wife, Louise, and my family for their unwavering patience and encouragement throughout the many hours of research and writing that brought this project to life.

CHAPTER ONE
Early Life

Charles L. Josselyn 1885 and in later years

Lewis Josselyn was born on September 13, 1883, in National City, San Diego. His birth was announced in *The Record*, a local newspaper in National City.[1] He is the father of Charles Lewis Josselyn (1850-1917) and Alice Roancy Lamb (1864-1944).

Charles Lewis Josselyn (1850-1917), was born on May 16, 1850, in Brookfield, Massachusetts. As the youngest of eight children in a modest New England family, he grew up with five brothers and two sisters. Charles went on to become an early pioneer in the fields of real estate, railroads, and mining.[2] [3]

Charles's father, George Dwelley Josselyn (1803-1858), was a shoemaker, and his mother, Alice Walker (1808-1855), was a housewife. Charles was the great-grandson of Charles Josselyn (1739-1812), who served as a private in Captain Thomas Turner's company of the Massachusetts Militia.[4] He fought in the battle of Bunker Hill during the Siege of Boston on April 19, 1775, at the outset of the American Revolutionary War.[5] The Josselyn ancestry goes back to Henry Josselyn (1697-1787) and Hannah Oldham (1700-1774), who were from Scituate, Plymouth, Massachusetts Bay.[6]

On March 12, 1875, Charles, and his brother James Riley Josselyn (1843-1937), established a homestead on the eastern shores of East Lake Weir in southern Marion County, Florida. Together, they owned 160 acres on the lake's eastern shoreline. Charles sold the property in 1881. His brother James went on to develop the "Josselyn grapefruit," which was in Belleview, Florida.[7]

Charles married Alice R. Lamb on June 27, 1882, in Worcester, Massachusetts. In 1883, they moved from Massachusetts to San Diego, California, and settled in National City, a town in the southwestern part of San Diego, where Charles was a real estate agent.[8]

In 1883, Charles bought 2 1/2 acres in Rancho de la Nacion, an old Mexican land grant situated in San Diego County.[9] In 1889, he acquired an additional 20 more acres in Rancho de la Nacion for $25,000.

Even after relocating to San Diego, Charles continued to make trips back east. His second son, Talbert, was born during one of these visits in Worcester, Massachusetts, on January 9, 1886.[10]

Charles was a member of the South West Masonic Lodge F. & A. M., of National City.[11] On September 15, 1886, he and other Masons gathered in Grange Hall on National Avenue for their first meeting.[12]

By 1887, the Josselyn family were
living at 425 Shell Avenue, in
Paradise Valley east of National City.
The Charles Josselyn House,
formerly known as the *House of Seven
Gables*, is a three-story Victorian
home built in 1889, perched on a hill
overlooking San Diego's South Bay.[13]
Josselyn purchased the lemon and
orange orchards for $500,000,
marking his shift from rancher and mine owner to citrus grower.[14]

425 Shell Avenue, National City

At age 7, while living in National City, their son Lewis Josselyn
was involved in a serious accident. While playing with some other
boys near a horse, the animal kicked him, breaking his arm and
shoulder. A local doctor set his bones.[15]

That same year, in 1889, Charles planned to construct a railroad
extending from the National City & Otay line to Tijuana. The
length of the road was 15 miles.[16] In 1893, Charles, with several San
Diego businessmen, established the San Diego, Fort Yuma and
Atlantic Railway Company.[17]

In 1895, Charles acquired a two-thirds stake in the Silver King
Mine, situated in the Picacho mining district near Yuma, Arizona.[18]
The following year, in 1896, he became a director of the Gold Basin
Mining and Milling Company, headquartered in San Diego.[19] On
April 20, 1896, Charles became the owner of the Guiding Star
Mining Claim for a group of copper and gold mines in the Copper
Mountains in Yuma County, Arizona.[20] [21] [22]

By the late 1890s, Charles and the family moved to 1544 5th Avenue

The Josselyn two-story home at 1546 A Street in San Diego

in downtown San Diego. In 1901 and 1902, Charles, Alice, and their three sons lived in a two-story house at 1546 A Street, San Diego.

On April 22, 1903, Lewis, age 19, went with his family on the steamship *Queen,* arriving in San Francisco after vacationing in Victoria, British Columbia.[23]

From 1904 to 1907, the family was listed as living on Brant Street near the corner of west Spruce Street in San Diego, California.[24]

In 1905, C. L. Josselyn returned from a five-week trip to the Death Valley mining region. In an interview, Josselyn said that "many people are taking up claims in the Funeral Mountain range country."[25] The Funeral Mountains is a mountain range along the California-Nevada border.

In 1909, the family traveled to Coronado, California and stayed in Tent City a popular amusement park. They occupied tent #2402 and were reported as bathing every day.[26]

Early in 1910, Lewis and his family arrived in New York City sailing from Southampton, England on the SS *Oceanic.*[27] *That same year,* the U.S. Census recorded the Josselyn family living in San Diego with Charles (59), Alice R. (45), Lewis (25), Talbert (24), and Winsor age (18). Interestingly, the census recorded the children's occupations as miners, their industry as gold, and their father's occupation as "own income."[28]

Later in 1910, the Josselyn family relocated to Berkeley before eventually settling in Pasadena, California.[29]

Charles passed away January 12, 1917, at his residence at 1749 North Raymond Avenue, Pasadena. His interment was in Pasadena.[30] [31]

After their father's death, their mother, Alice, joined her three sons who were already living in Carmel.[32] Their father's will was filed for probate on December 12, 1917. Josselyn and his two brothers, Talbert and Winsor, inherited $120,000 (equivalent to $2,853,818 in 2023). The estate primarily consisted of United States 3% Liberty Bonds, including $20,00 in U.S. bonds issued in 1898.[33] [34]

Alice R. Lamb

Alice Josselyn in 1920 and her father Jairus B. Lamb

Lewis's mother, Alice Roancy Lamb (1864-1944), was born on June 10, 1864, in Worcester, Massachusetts. She was one of four children born to Jarius B. Lamb (1833-1913) and Harriet A. Severance (1833-1900).[35]

Alice grew up in Worcester, Massachusetts, where she lived with her parents and worked as a bookkeeper at the age of 16. After marrying Charles Josselyn in 1882, she left Massachusetts, and the couple moved to San Diego in 1883.

During World War I, while her two sons were serving in the war, she began her lifelong work in the Red Cross, where she introduced the making of scrapbooks and separately bound magazine stories for the use of hospitalized Veteran soldiers. [36]

Alice was actively engaged in community affairs, contributing to the early formation of the Forest Theater and the Abalone League in Carmel-by-the-Sea.[37] She was the first official scorer for the League.[38]

In late 1919, Alice purchased nearly all the Carmel lots near the Forest Theater in blocks 81 and 82, with the exception of lot 26, from the Carmel Development Company for $10.[39]

By early 1920, the U.S. Census showed the family living on Casanova Street in Carmel. Alice, 54, was joined by her sons: Lewis, 36, a photographer; Talbert, 33, an author; and Winsor, 24.[40]

Alice built a house for herself on Guadalupe Street (lots 5, 7, & 9) in 1921 for $6,000, near Ocean Avenue.

In June 1925 Alice was in San Francisco and saw in the production of *The Rivals*, with actress Minnie Maddern Fiske in the leading role.[41]

Alice moved to Monterey in 1941. In Monterey she was involved in the Monterey Civic Club and the Cascarone Ball.[42] [43]

Alice Josselyn died at her home on January 31, 1944, in Monterey. Private funeral services were held at the Howell Mission Chapel in Monterey.[44] [45]

Talbert Josselyn

Talbert Josselyn in 1910 and 1916, photos by Lewis Josselyn

Arthur Talbert Josselyn, known as "Tal," was the second son of Charles and Alice Josselyn, born on January 9, 1886, in Worcester, Massachusetts, during one of Charles's trips back east. Talbert grew up in San Diego and attended Stanford University from 1907-1909 and was a member of Stanford's Delta Tau Delta fraternity.[46] [47] In 1910, he attended the University of California at Berkeley as a Junior.[48] [49] [50]

On September 2, 1912, the *Oakland Tribune* reported on the 1910 graduates of the University of California, Berkeley, saying that Talbert Joselyn was engaged in literary work on Diamond Island, located off the coast of Maine.[51]

In 1914, Talbert and his brothers settled in the art colony of Carmel-by-the-Sea, California, where he wrote fiction for pulp magazines and became acquainted with many writers in Carmel.[52]

During World War I, on September 9, 1918, 32-year-old Talbert registered with the U.S. Army in Pasadena.[53] Although he didn't pass the physical requirements for service because of his eyesight, he contributed by joining the Massachusetts Farm Committee Camp program, where he served until being admitted to an officers' training program.[54] [55]

While his brothers were fighting in World War I, Talbert focused on pursuing a career in writing and acting. On January 16, 1919, he performed in a three-act play titled *The Private Secretary* at the Manzanita Theater in Carmel, taking on the role of "Mr. Marland."[56] Talbert took part in acting at the Forest Theater, the Theater of the Golden Bough, and the Carmel Arts and Crafts Club's Theater.[57]

Following World War I, Talbert gained national recognition as a writer of sports story and novels. His works appeared in prominent publications like *Collier's Magazine* and *Saturday Evening Post*. The Monterey Peninsula served as the backdrop for much of his writing.

On August 6, 1927, Talbert married Florence Mullen Thorton (1897-1992), at the Berkeley Unitarian Church by Rev. Vander Lann. His brother Winsor was best man. For their honeymoon, they traveled on the S.S. *Alexander* and visited Seattle, Glacier National Park, the Canadian Rockies, and Yellowstone. Florence was previously married to a Thorton but was divorced by the time she met Talbert.[58] [59] [60]

Florence was born on September 29, 1897, in Gilroy, California, as Florence Bison Mullen, the daughter of James Monroe Mullen (1849-1923) and Florence Cordelia Serles (1860-1906).[61] She was known for her contributions to civic affairs as a founding member of the Carmel Planning Commission, serving from 1947 to 1996.

She was a member of the Carmel City Council from 1973 to 1976, where she also served as police commissioner. Florence was on the Harrison Memorial library board for six years. She taught at the Sunset School in Carmel from 1923 to 1927 and spent 17 years teaching sixth grade at Seaside School before retiring in 1957.[62] [63]

Talbert and Florence had one child, a daughter named Barbara Josselyn, who was born on January 3, 1929, in Carmel-by-the-Sea and later resided in Piedmont, California.[64] [65] Barbara went to Carmel High School and then went to Berkeley from 1947 to 1950. She lived in the UC campus Stern Hall dormitory.[66] Barbara married Maurice Asa in May 1957 in Alameda County.[67] and had two children together, David (born in 1959) and Rachel (born 1961).[68]

In 1935, Talbert and his wife Florence built their family home on Santa Rita Street, near the Forest Theater in Carmel.[69] According to the 1940 U.S. Census, the family was still living there. Talbert, then age 54 years old, lived with Florence, age 42, and their 11-year-old daughter Barbara.[70]

Second Wind (1940) by Talbert Josselyn, courtesy of
Saturday Evening Post

Warner Brothers purchased the movie rights for Talbert's story "Second Wind," published as "Kunming Cargo" in *Saturday Evening Post* on Jan 27, 1940, though the film was never released.[71] In 1942, his article *Courage Beyond Duty* was published in *This Week* magazine. During World War II, Talbert was assigned to the Office of War Information in San Francisco and edited the final draft of the "Strategic Bombing of Japan Survey."[72]

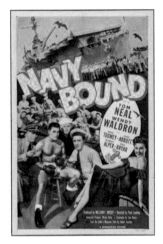

On February 26, 1943, Talbert wrote an article for the *Monterey Peninsula Herald* called "Monterey Patrol," where he was assigned by the Navy Section Base at Monterey to do a story about an overnight patrol off the California coast.[73]

After World War II, Talbert became known for writing *Smuggler's Cove* (1948) and *Navy Bound* (1951), both of which were adapted into films and released by Monogram Pictures. He completed a western novel published by the Chicago Tribune-New York New Syndicate, titled *Golden City*.[74]

In the 1950s, Josselyn continued to write and travel. In June 1953, he wrote the article "Green Valley," for *The Country Guide*.[75] In April 1956, the family traveled to Paradise Valley and Scottsdale, Arizona.[76]

Talbert died at his Santa Rita Street home in Carmel on April 2, 1961, at the age of 76. Private funeral services were held at the Little Chapel-by-the-Sea in Pacific Grove, officiated by Dr. J. M. Ewing, minister of the Carmel Presbyterian Church.[77] [78] His wife, Florence, died 31 years later, on May 29, 1992, at the age of 95, also

at their Santa Rita Street home. A private cremation took place at
the Little Chapel by-the-Sea, in Pacific Grove.[79]

Winsor Josselyn

Winsor Josselyn was born on September
17, 1895, in San Diego. He was the
youngest child of Charles and Alice
Josselyn.[80]

Winsor entered service for World War I
at Pasadena on May 21, 1917, in the
ambulance Corps #1, and went on to
Camp Crane in Allentown,
Pennsylvania, and then Base Hospital 34,
in Nantes, France.[81]

Winsor Josselyn, circa 1915,
photo by Lewis Josselyn

Winsor wrote the *Carmel Pine Cone* a
letter that was posted on July 5, 1917, from the U. S. Army Hospital
Ambulance Corps Training Camp in Allentown, Pennsylvania. He
talked about army camp life, converting a fairground into sleeping,
living quarters, and getting the necessary training to prepare for
his departure to France in August.[82]

Winsor served overseas in France during World War I alongside
his brother Lewis. He was stationed with the French army in
Picardy, near the Cigogné airfield, where René Fonck, the
renowned fighter ace, was based.[83]

On April 10, 1918, while serving at Base Hospital 34, Winsor joined
the lead surgical team when Major Ashurst left for the front.
Winsor contributed several chapters to the book *Base Hospital 34 in
the World War*, published in Philadelphia in July 1922. The chapters
he wrote included "On Detached Service: Brest," "Surgical Team

No. 23: Introduction," "St. Nazaire to New York," and "Camp Merritt and Camp Dix."[84]

In 1919, Winsor was listed as going to Stanford University.[85] A family photo shows a group shot of him with his Stanford fraternity brothers.

Windsor wrote World War I short stories, was an inventor, and a broadcaster for *The Pine Cone's* KRML station. In 1928, he and his brother Talbert co-wrote an article titled "Dry Water" for *Popular Magazine*, which centered on a small-town storekeeper.[86]

Winsor also ventured into newspaper work in Carmel in the early 1930s with a brief stint at the *San Francisco Examiner*.[87] He wrote articles for the *Carmel Pine Cone* and, in February 1931, wrote an article about the Abalone League.[88] He contributed to an article on Jo Mora to *California Arts and Architecture*. The piece was illustrated with half-tone photographs of Mora's sculptures and included descriptions of his studies.[89] In 1933 he wrote for The *Californian*.[90] Between 1935, and up to World War II, Winsor wrote for the *Monterey Herald*.[91]

As an inventor, Winsor filed patents for pruning shears (1946), cigarette holders (1919), a brush (1931), and tape dispensers (1948).[92] [93]

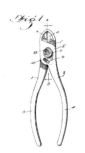

Pruning shears (1946) patent

On February 24, 1939, Winsor interviewed former Carmel mayor Allen Knight and wrote about "The Ship," the house Knight built that year, in the *Monterey Peninsula Herald*. Describing his creation, Knight remarked, "The building resembled a stone lighthouse. Some people call this my hobby…and some people call it my marine mania. Call it what you will, but I love ships and I'm getting a big kick out of doing it."[94]

In 1939, Winsor learned to fly at the Monterey airport (now the Monterey Regional Airport). He got his private license in 1940.[95]

In 1940, Winsor wrote an article in *Harper's Magazine* titled "He Flew in 1883," highlighting the pioneering glider experiments conducted by Professor John Joseph Montgomery of Santa Clara University in Santa Clara in California. These historic aviation achievements, which marked a major milestone in controlled flight, took place in 1883.[96]

Winsor married Merle Luella Larritt (1905-1993) on April 12, 1942, in La Jolla, California, at the home of her parents.[97] They had one child, Gertrude "Trudy" Alice Josselyn, born on September 3, 1947, in San Diego, California.[98] Trudy attended Westmoor High School in Daily City, California,[99] and later went on to study at San Jose State University. On October 27, 1974, Trudy later married Charles M. Salter at the Forest Theater, with a reception at the Pine Inn.[100] [101]

In my interview with Trudy, she shared memories of visiting her Uncle Lewis with her father when she was a teenager. She vividly remembered seeing him at the Monterey County Fair, proudly wearing his American Legion cap. Trudy also reminisced about Lewis's home on Santa Rita Street in Carmel, particularly his darkroom located in the downstairs basement.

In 1942, age 46, Winsor was living at the Press Club at 5700 Sutter and Powell Streets in San Francisco. In May 1942, he was commissioned as a first lieutenant in the U.S. Army Air Force during World War II. He served as a public relations writer for the military at Fort Mason and was promoted to captain in July 1943.[102] [103]

In 1944, Captain Winsor served with the Fourth Fighter Command, headquartered in Oakland, California.[104]

Winsor Josselyn was stationed at Kunming, China, with the U.S. Army Air Force public relations department.[105]

The U.S. 1950 Census listed Winsor and his family as living in Alhambra, Los Angeles County, California, Winsor, age 54, Merle, age 44, and daughter Gertrude A. Josselyn, age 2. Winsor was listed in public relations for the Veterans Service.[106] In the 1950s, Winsor worked in public relations for the Navel Ordnance Test Center in Temple City, Los Angeles, California.

When Winsor retired in the mid 60's he worked part time at Fort Mason in San Francisco and lived on 95 Lake Meadow Drive in Daily City in the Westlake neighborhood. He enjoyed woodworking, golf, and reading.

Winsor died on June 14, 1973, at Valley Park Convalescent Hospital in Mill Valley, California, Marin County, at age 77. He was cremated at Cypress Lawn in Coma City.[107] On November 30, 1993, his wife, Merle, died in Walnut Creek, California. They were both buried together and share the same headstone at the Golden Gate National Cemetery.[108] [109]

Education

Lewis Josselyn (1900) Boston, Massachusetts

In 1896, at the age of 13, Lewis Josselyn began attending high school in San Diego. After completing high school in 1900, he pursued his passion for art and photography by enrolling at the Eric Pape School of Art in Boston, Massachusetts. Founded and directed by the renowned artist Eric Pape, the school was known for its rigorous curriculum.[110]

Josselyn was part of a vibrant artistic community that included future luminaries like Maynard Dixon, celebrated for his iconic depictions of the American West, and Howard Pyle, often regarded as the father of American illustration. These formative years laid the foundation for his future contributions to the art world.[111] [112]

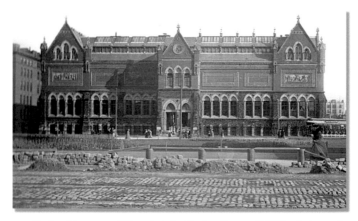

Boston Museum of Fine Arts in Copley Square (1900), photograph by Lewis Josselyn

While studying at art school in Boston, Josselyn captured photographs of notable landmarks such as the Boston Museum of Fine Art in Copley Square, as well as the Arlington Street Church across from the Public Garden in Boston.

Massachusetts State Building (1900), photograph by Lewis Josselyn

Josselyn photographed Massachusetts State Building, situated in Boston's historic Beacon Hill neighborhood. This photograph is an early example of Josselyn's ability to document significant cultural landmarks of Massachusetts. [113]

Early Years

Josselyn's passion for photography led him to travel extensively, capturing images of diverse locations across the United States. Among his earliest known works are a photograph of the Sweetwater Dam, located 12 miles east of San Diego, during its dramatic overflow in 1900.[114]

On July 7, 1901, Josselyn captured the head-on collision between two passenger trains at Black Butte Summit located in northern California, near the town of Weed in Siskiyou County. The incident was caused by a switch failure or miscommunication.[115] Newspaper articles about the train crash appeared in publications like *The San Francisco Chronicle* and *The San Francisco Call and Post*.[116]

In 1904, Josselyn photographed Ocean Beach, located north of Point Loma, San Diego.
The next year, he captured an image of "The Poet's Walk" at Chapultepec Park in Mexico City, which was featured in *The Burr McIntosh Monthly*. The path is lined by trees that are centuries old.[117]

In 1908, Josselyn captured images of the gateway to the Theosophical Society buildings in Point Loma, San Diego, as well as the battleships of *Great White Fleet* off the coast of Southern California.[118]

Poet's Walk" at Chapultepec Park, Mexico City (1916), photo by Josselyn

On April 22, 1911, Lewis Josselyn

applied for membership with the Sons of the American Revolution as a descendent of Charles Josselyn. In the application he was listed as a rancher in Phoenix, Arizona.[119]

Tal, Lewis, and Winsor - Christmas 1913

In February 1913, one of the last events before moving to Carmel was when Lewis and Talbert attended the 1913 engagement party for Mildred Whitman (1890-1960) and Munro Montgomery (1890-1957) in Los Angeles. The couple was known for their involvement in the early 20th-century cultural and artist scene.[120] [121]

Carmel-by-the-Sea

John Martin Ranch, photo by Lewis Josselyn

In November 1914, the Josselyn family settled in the art colony of Carmel-by-the-Sea, California, where Josselyn became one of the town's first commercial photographers. One of his first notable images of Carmel was a photograph of the John Martin Ranch on the north side of the Carmel River, known today as Mission Ranch.[122]

During this time, Josselyn also formed a friendship with fellow commercial photographer Louis S. Slevin, who had moved to Carmel in 1903 and established a general merchandise store that sold curios, stationary, magazines, and photographic supplies.

In December 1914, Lewis, Winsor, and Talbert all attended a weekend dance with other Carmelites hosted at the home of Mrs. A. Hale in Carmel.[123]

Carmel Beach looking towards Carmel Point and Point Lobos (1925)
photo by Lewis Josselyn.[124]

On May 26, 1915, Josselyn, his father, and his brothers embarked on a ten-day camping trip in the San Antonio Valley in eastern Santa Clara County. After the trip, Winsor and their father continued traveling south, while Josselyn and Talbert returned home.[125]

During the Christmas season of 1915, Josselyn sold 1916 art calendars and mounted pictures featuring local scenes, which could be purchased at the Pine Cone office and the Blue Bird Tea Room.[126]

1915 Add for Calendars in the
Carmel Pine Cone

In 1915, Josselyn began photographing plays at the Forest Theater where his brothers, Winsor and Talbert started taking on acting roles. We will explore this further in the next chapter, "Theater Work." The following year, in January 1916, Josselyn attended a farewell surprise party for actor and director Herbert Heron who was heading to Los Angeles. Among the other attendees were actors Katherine Cooke, Philip Wilson, and George Schweninger.[127]

In early September 1916, Josselyn went on several hikes with the Carmel Boys' Club. One hike started at Monte Verde Street in Carmel for a 40-minute hike to a eucalyptus grove and a "Good Times Pool." They met Frank. Devendorf in his "machine" and the boys then went sailing.[128] Another hike led to Pescadero Canyon, where the boys were given notebooks to record observations of birds, trees, plants, flowers, and animal tracks.[129]

Cypress Trees

Monterey cypress tree (1920s), photos by Lewis Josselyn.

Josselyn's images of Monterey cypress trees gained widespread recognition and appeared in numerous publications. In 1916, Josselyn photographed the iconic Lone Cypress, a Monterey cypress tree located at Midway Point along the 17-Mile Drive in Pebble Beach.[130] [131]

Lone Cypress Midway Point, Pebble Beach (1916) photo
by Lewis Josselyn

His photograph of a Monterey cypress was featured as the frontispiece in poet Julia Boynton Green's 1928 book, *This Enchanting Coast*.[132]

His work also captured the beauty of the trees in Carmel Valley.[133]

In November 1916, Josselyn traveled to Pasadena to be with his mother and father for the holidays.[134]

In March 1917, Josselyn and two buglers led members of the Carmel Boys' Club on a hike to Pinchot Peak in the Carmel Highlands. Each boy kept an "observation" notebook where they recorded the names of flowers, trees, and insects, fostering their ability to observe and learn from their surroundings. The outing was recorded as "Club Notes," written in the *Carmel Pine Cone* by painter Johnson,[135] who played a role in establishing the Carmel Art Association, the Carmel Boys' Club, and Carmel's first free library.[136]

World War I

Josselyn (far right) at X-Ray Department, ca. 1917

On May 6, 1917, Josselyn, age 34, departed Carmel with his 22-year-old brother Winsor and their mother for Pasadena. There they enlisted in the U.S. Army Medical Corps at the onset of World War I.[137]

By May 21, 1917, both Winsor and Lewis had registered with the World War I Selective Service System,[138] and entered service with Ambulance Corps #1 in Pasadena. During this time, the brothers reportedly visited Los Angeles, where they attended several notable social events.[139]

Their mother bid them farewell in Pasadena as they embarked for Camp Crane in Allentown, Pennsylvania. At Camp Crane, they joined the Pasadena No. 1 Ambulance Corps,[140] which served as a training hub for the United States Army Ambulance Service (USAAS).[141]

On December 15, 1917, Lewis and Winsor departed from Hoboken, New Jersey, aboard the ship *Leviathan*, bound for Base Hospital No. 34 in France as part of the 41 St Division.[142]

Both brothers served as privates first class from May 21, 1917, to July 21, 1919. By January 10, 1918, The *Carmel Pine Cone* reported that the Josselyn brothers had arrived in France,[143] where they were stationed at Base Hospital No. 34 in Nantes. Lewis took on multiple roles, serving as an ambulance driver, cook, and assistant in the X-ray department.[144] He was later promoted from private to corporal within the ambulance service.[145]

General Pershing visit to Base Hospital 34 (1918) by Lewis Josselyn

While serving at the base hospital, Josselyn photographed the American Expeditionary Forces. His war photography included capturing General John J. Pershing's visit to Base Hospital 34, in 1918, as well as images of the surgical Ward, X-ray department, and the army kitchen at the hospital. Lewis was on the editorial staff for the book, *Base Hospital 34 in the World War*, which was published in Philadelphia in July 1922.[146] He traveled extensively throughout France, capturing photographs for the French government.[147]

On June 23, 1919, Lewis departed St. Nazaire, France on the ship *Wilhelmina*, and arrived in Hoboken, New Jersey on July 3, 1919.

His ship registration said that he was in the museum unit No. 1, photographic division, medical department.[148]

In 1919, Josselyn was able to travel to Salt Lake City, Utah, where he photographed the Brigham Young Monument, a bronzed historical monument located at the intersection at Main and South Temple Streets.[149]

Augustine Jeanne Richard

While recovering from injuries at the army hospital in Nantes, France, Lewis met and fell in love with a nurse named Augustine Jeanne Richard (1896-1988),[150] who went by her middle name, "Jeanne."

Jeanne Josselyn 1923, U.S. passport photo

Jeanne was born on May 16, 1896, in Nantes, France. She was a homemaker and was an active member of the Alliance Française, an organization dedicated to promoting the French language and culture.[151]

Her parents were Jean Marie Richard (1863-1955) and Marie Joséphine Bernard (1860-1903), who were married on January 14, 1887, in Nantes, Loire-Inférieure, France.[152]

On February 24, 1920, Augustine Jeanne Richard and Lewis Josselyn were married in Manhattan, New York City. Their marriage record included the names of their parents.[153] Following the ceremony, a reception and dinner were held at the home of Calvin H. Luther in Stamford, Connecticut. Luther, a close family friend, later relocated to Carmel, where he pursued acting, appearing in the play, *Mr. Bunt,* and remained in Carmel for years. The couple stayed in Stamford for a few days before embarking on their honeymoon, which included visits to the Grand Canyon and Pasadena.[154] By March 18th, Josselyn's mother and his two brothers joined the newlyweds in Pasadena.[155]

On March 2, 1924, Lewis and his wife celebrated their fourth wedding anniversary with friends at the Blue Bird Tearoom.[156]

On October 25, 1928, Lewis, 44, and his wife, 33, returned to New York aboard the SS *President Roosevelt,* after departing from Cherbourg, France.[157]

In 1930, Jeanne taught French at the Carmel Academy of Music and Fine Arts. In 1932, Jeanne sailed to France for six months to visit family and relatives.[158]

In the 1940s, Jeanne was involved in Helene Vye's Little Shop to develop a French atmosphere called *Les Galeries Lafayettes.*[159]

In 1953, she participated in Bastille Day held at the Carmel Art Gallery. She guided the guests through a selection of nostalgic French ballads.[160]

Jeanne died on December 2, 1987, at her home in Carmel. Funeral services were held on December 30th at the Blessed Sacrament Chapel of the Carmel Mission. She was cremated at the Little Chapel by-the-Sea, and her remains were buried alongside her husband at the Golden Gate National Cemetery in San Bruno.[161]

Post-War Era

Coming back to Carmel after the war, Lewis and Winsor became honorary life members of the American Legion Post #41 of Monterey in 1919.[162] They were also enrolled on the Carmel voter index as "Republican."[163]

In 1919, Josselyn's mother purchased land near the Forest Theater from the Carmel Development Company. At the time, the family was living in a house on Casanova Street in Carmel.[164]

On February 5, 1920, the *Carmel Pine Cone* reported that Josselyn was working to cultivate the land his mother purchased near the Forest Theater by planting fruit trees. He took advantage of holes created by dynamite blasts on the four acres she had acquired.[165]

Family Camping in 1921, photographed by Lewis Josselyn.

The California U.S. Voter Registration for 1920 listed the Josselyn family along with other artists and writers living in Carmel. For example, the registry listed writer James M. Hopper, artist Ida A. Johnson, and hotel proprietor Mary L. Hamlin.[166]

By 1921, Carmel was still a small town. Josselyn captured a photograph of a family camping and cooking at the corner of Ocean Avenue and Guadalupe Street, as they waited for their newly purchased lots to be developed into cottages.[167]

Lewis, Winsor, and Talbert were actively engaged in Carmel's social and political scene. In the 1920s, the *Monterey Daily Cypress and Monterey American* featured a section called "Latest News from Carmel by the Sea," highlighting local social events. One such occasion in August 1922, was a dance hosted by Mr. and Mrs. Lee Gottfried at their home on Dolores Street. Gottfried was a builder credited with reintroducing the use of Carmel stone as a local building material. Guests included Mr. and Mrs. Edward Kuster, Mr. and Mrs. Hobart Glassell, Winsor Josselyn, Talbert Josselyn, Mr. and Mrs. Lewis Josselyn, Mr. and Mrs. Frederick Bechdolt, Mr. and Mrs. John Northern Hilliard, Harrison Goldwin, Ernest Schweinger, and Katherine Cook, among others.[168]

Solar eclipse in Lompoc, California (1923), photo by Lewis Josselyn

On September 10, 1923, Lewis and Winsor went to Lompoc, in Santa Barbara County, California, to photograph the solar eclipse with Professor Burton, Evan Mosher, and James Worthington.

On separate occasions in 1924 and again in 1925, the *Oakland Tribune* reported that Josselyn and his wife attended dinner parties at the home of Mr. and Mrs. John Northern Hilliard at Eighty Acres.[169] [170]

Carmel Arts and Crafts Club

Carmel Arts and Crafts Club

From August 9 to September 4, 1920, Josselyn, alongside fellow photographer Louis S. Slevin and other artists, showcased their photographs and paintings at the Fourteenth Annual Art Exhibition. The event was hosted by the Carmel Arts and Crafts Club, a gallery, theater, and clubhouse established in 1905 in Carmel-by-the-Sea. Among the thirty-eight participating artists were Charlton Fortune and Mary DeNeale Morgan.[171] Josselyn submitted a collection of historical war photos and images depicting scenes from Carmel to the exhibition. Josselyn was among the Monterey artists highlighted by the Carmel Arts and Crafts Club in its promotion for national recognition.[172] [173]

In September 1925, Josselyn exhibited his work beyond the Monterey Peninsula by participating in the Pacific International Photographers' Association's first annual international convention, held at the Fairmont Hotel in San Francisco.[174] [175] [176]

Abalone League

*Abalone League with aviator Virginia Stanton and Wilna
Hervey (1922) by Lewis Josselyn*

After World War I the Abalone League baseball games gained
popularity. In the early 1920s, Josselyn was actively involved in
both photography and playing in the league. The games were held
on a bluff at Carmel Point, near Carmel. Thorne Taylor and writer
Talbert Josselyn co-founded the Abalone League, which became
the first softball league in the Western United States. Talbert
helped develop the rules for the game.[177]

Josselyn and his wife became part of a community of writers and
artists. The games were held in a rough diamond field among the
pine trees overlooking the rocky coastline near the home of Charles
King Van Riper, one of Carmel's story writers.[178]

In 1922, actress and writer Katherine Cooke wrote in the *Oakland
Tribune* about the Abalone League, highlighting, "Mr. and Mrs.
Lewis Josselyn, the latter notable because she is the swiftest runner
of all the women."[179]

The following year, the *Tribune* again featured the league, emphasizing its famous writers and artists. The article mentioned Charles Van Riper, a successful Carmel's story writers, John Northern Hilliard novelist, director, and star first baseman, and Leon Wilson, author of *Merton of the Movies*. It also mentioned Byington Ford, Del Monte hotel manager, Herbert Heron, Carmel's poet and actor, Lewis Josselyn, an artist, and his petite French wife, who became the league's expert scorekeeper. Talbert Josselyn, a short story writer, was noted for umpiring the final game.[180]

Passports to Travel

In September 1923, Josselyn and his wife, Jeanne, embarked on a journey to Europe. To facilitate their travel, they applied for U.S. passports, a process that required credible individuals to vouch for their identities. Jeanne's identity was affirmed by two close family members and friends: Salmon F. Dutton and her mother-in-law, Alice Josselyn. Similarly, Lewis's

Lewis Josselyn 1932 Passport Photo

application was supported by his brother, Winsor Josselyn, and his mother. Lewis stayed in Europe for three months, dedicating his time to capturing images and documenting the World War I reconstruction process to rebuild war-torn regions. Meanwhile, Jeanne extended her stay to six months, using the additional time to visit relatives.[181] [182] [183]

Three years later, on June 13, 1926, Lewis and Jeanne traveled to France, where she planned to spent time with her parents. Meanwhile, Lewis continued on to Africa to join a group of friends from Pasadena for a big-game hunting expedition.[184]

Maritime Photography

USS Mount Vernon (1917-1919) and Schooner Flavel (1923), photos by Lewis Josselyn

Josselyn gained recognition for his maritime photography, including documenting his time in the Army. He had the opportunity to photograph the U.S. USS *Mount Vernon*, which played a role as a U.S. Army troop transport ship. Josselyn's photographs captured the ship in port, during its operations.[185]

On December 14, 1923, Josselyn photographed the steam schooner Flavel, which ran aground in dense fog near Cypress Point in Pebble Beach. It was carrying lumber from Aberdeen, Washington to San Pedro, California.[186] [187]

Oil tanker Frank H. Buck (1924) photo by Lewis Josselyn

Josselyn documented two dramatic events involving the Associated Oil Company in 1924. On May 3, 1924, he photographed the grounding of the 427-foot-long oil tanker *Frank H. Buck* on the rocks at Point Pinos in Pacific Grove, California.[188] [189]

Later, on September 14, he captured images of the devastating fire that erupted when lightning struck one of the company's oil tanks, leading to the destruction of the entire tank facility.[190]

On October 1, 1933, Josselyn photographed the USS *Constitution*, also known as *Old Ironsides*, as it sailed through Monterey Bay. This three-masted, wooden-hulled heavy frigate of the United States Navy is a celebrated symbol of American maritime history.[191]

Yosemite

Yosemite Falls and a giant sequoia redwood, photos by Lewis Josselyn

Yosemite became a popular destination for photographers and tourists in the 1920s. On June 21, 1925, the Oakland Tribune reported that Lewis and Jeanne were planning to visit Yosemite Valley, where he captured photographs of the road to Yosemite, its majestic waterfalls, and redwoods.[192]

In 1930, he photographed the California Tunnel Tree, a giant sequoia redwood in the Mariposa Grove of Yosemite National Park, with a base enough for vehicles to drive through.[193]

Santa Rita Street

In 1919, Josselyn's mother purchased blocks 81 and 82 near the Forest Theater from the Carmel Development Company.[194] She and her sons donated a strip of land providing access from the Santa Rita Road to the entrance gates of the Forest Theater through a deed of gift.[195] In 1981, the city approved the naming of a path connecting Santa Rita Street to Guadalupe Street at the north end of the Forest Theater property as Josselyn Lane, in honor of the Josselyn family of Carmel, who donated a portion of the land.[196]

This area, known as the Eighty-Acre Tract, is notable for the Flanders Mansion, a property listed on the National Register of Historic Places. Josselyn photographed the mansion in 1926 (see Chapter Six on Buildings).[197]

In 1926, Josselyn purchased four acres of land (lots 17-25, block 81) from his mother, Alice, for $10.00. Located at the corner of Santa Rita Street and 7th Avenue in Carmel, near the Forest Theater between Ocean Avenue and Mountain View Avenue, this property became the site for his family home and photographic studio. Josselyn built their residence on lots 17-19.[198]

By 1930, the Josselyn family was firmly established in their Santa Rita Street home. According to the U.S. Census that year, Lewis, aged 45, worked as a photographer, while Jeanne, 33 and originally from France, managed their household. The couple owned the property, which was valued at $6,000.[199]

Lewis's brother Talbert and his wife, Florence, bought property across the street at Santa Rita Street 6 on block 82, lots 14, 16, 18, on the east side of Santa Rita Street. The property is considered historic for its association with the writer Talbert Josselyn.[200] The house is a two-story stucco building built in 1935 by local building contractor A. Carlyle Stoney. The residence is situated back from Santa Rita Street on a high knoll, behind a redwood grape-stake fence. It has unobstructed views of Carmel Bay and Point Lobos.[201]

In 1940, Talbert built a Vernacular-style house on lot 20, on Santa Rita Street 8 just south of his lot 16-18 house. It boarders along Josselyn Trail (7th Street), north of the Forest Theater. A second story bedroom above the one-car garage was added in 1943.[202]

The Talbert Josselyn House on Santa Rita Street, Lot 20

The 1940 U.S. Census records the Lewis Josselyn family residing on Santa Rita Street in Carmel. Lewis was 55 years old, and Augustine was 42.[203]

In 1948, Talbert also built a two-story house on Santa Rita 4 (block 82, Lot 8) southeast of Ocean Avenue as a rental or as a spec house and later sold it to Werner G. Pundt.[204]

Barbara Josselyn Asa House on Santa Rita Street, Lot 21

In 1932, Lewis Josselyn built a second two-story house for $2,000, on lot 21, block 81, located on the west side of Santa Rita Street, just south of his lot 17-19, near 7th Avenue, across from the Forest Theater. He sold this property on June 1, 1933, to M. J. Murphy for $550.00.[205] This house later owned and became known as the Barbara Josselyn Asa Property.[206]

On October 8, 2004, the *Carmel Pine Cone* reported the sale of the Barbara J. Asa home sale on Santa Rita & Mountain View 3NE for $1,500.000 to the Santa Rita LLC.[207]

The properties were included in a survey conducted by the Carmel Preservation Foundation between 1989 and 1991, which found the residence significant due to its association with Lewis Josselyn. The properties remained in the family trust until Florence's death on May 29, 1992. The property has since been transferred to her daughter, Barbara Josselyn Asa, as trustee.[208]

CHAPTER TWO
Theater Work

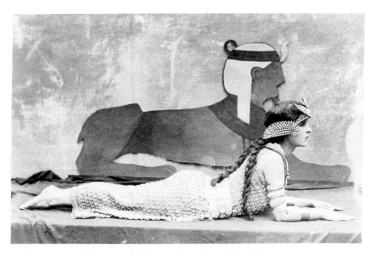

Caesar and Cleopatra (1922) by Lewis Josselyn

Forest Theater

As the official photographer for the Forest Theater, Lewis Josselyn captured dramatic images of its actors, sets, and productions. His connections with local artists and writers gave him unique access to the theater's creative community. This outdoor amphitheater in Carmel-by-the-Sea, California, was a key venue for artistic expression and cultural events in the area, celebrated for its natural setting and distinctive outdoor performances. The theater hosted a wide range of productions, including works by local artists and theatrical groups like the Western Drama Society, with which Josselyn had a close association.

Lewis Josselyn captured a range of live theatrical productions, including Robert Louis Stevenson's *Tusitala* (1916), *Inchling* (1922), *Caesar and Cleopatra* (1922), and *Hamlet* (1926). Alongside his work as a photographer, Josselyn also served as a stage manager and oversaw stage lighting for various theater's productions.[209]

Junipero Serra

Josselyn took some of his first theatrical photographs for the Sixth Annual production at the Forest Theater for the play *Junípero Serra*, which ran from July 2-5, 1915. Winsor and Talbert Josselyn participated as dancers. Written by Perry Newberry *Junípero Serra* was a historical pageant-drama highlighting the life of Father Junípero Serra.[210]

Junípero Serra (1915) photo by Josselyn

Talbert wrote in the *Carmel Pine Cone*, "Here was a play worthy of the setting among oaks and pines—it had sweep and movements, massed groups and color and pageantry— Here was the whole community giving its effort, and summer people as well."[211]

On August 27-28, 1915, the play *The Pageant of Monterey*, based on the same *Junipero Serra*, which was presented in July at the Forest Theater, played at the Court of the Universe, Panama–Pacific International Exposition in San Francisco, with 400 actors and actresses. The production was under the direction of Perry Newberry.[212] In March 1915, Josselyn and his family had visited the Panama–Pacific International Exposition in San Francisco.[213]

Western Drama Society

A Midsummer Night's Dream, (1915), photo by
Lewis Josselyn

As tensions arose between directors Herbert Heron of the Forest
Theater and Perry Newberry, it led to a split. Newberry, along with
Edward Kuster, broke away to form the Western Drama Society in
1912. Founding members included George Sterling, Herbert Heron,
James Hopper, Jack London, and others. Plays produced by the
Western Drama Society included *Fire* (1913), *The Arrow Maker*
(1914), *Macaire* (1914), *Montezuma* (1914), *A Midsummer Night's
Dream* (1915), *The First Poet* (1915*)*, and *Tusitala* (1916*)*.[214]

On July 17, 1915, Josselyn photographed William Shakespeare's'
comedy play *A Midsummer Night's Dream,* performed at the Forest
Theater by the Western Drama Society. Talbert Josselyn played the
role of Robin Starveling the tailor. The play was directed by
Herbert Heron and Helen Parkes.[215] [216]

On July 19, 1915, the Western Drama Society held its third annual
production of new plays. Josselyn photographed the performances,
which included Jack London's *The First Poet*, a drama set in the
Stone Age. He also served as assistant stage manager for the Helen
Parkes' flower-fantasy *play, The Columbine*.[217] [218]

On August 7, 1915, Josselyn handled the photography for the play *The Man From Home,* written by Harry Leon Wilson and Booth Tarkington, at the Forest Theater. The comedy play with four acts was produced by Glenn Hughes for the Carmel Arts and Crafts Club. Talbert played the role of Mariano, while Winsor portrayed the young American, Horace Granger-Simpson.[219] [220]

The next year, alongside playwright Herbert Heron and John Northern Hilliard, Josselyn took on the role of officer and treasurer of the Western Drama Society.[221] By 1919, the Western Drama Society had merged into the Forest Theater. [222]

Tusitala

In July 1916, the Drama Society put on the fourth annual production with "Tusitala" on July 21st and 28th. The play was written by John Northern Hilliard and Herbert Heron with six episodes based on Robert Louis Stevenson's books: The Prologue, Episode 2: Treasure Island, Episode 3: The Black Arrow, Episode 4: The Treasure of Franchard, Episode 5: The Ebb Tide, and Episode 6: Weir of Hermiston. [223] [224]

Antonio Corsi in Tusitala
Treasure Island (1916)
photo by Josselyn

Josselyn took on the role of photographer and stage manager. His brother, Talbert, took the part of Huish for the episodes, *Treasure Island* and *The Ebb Tide.*[225]

The first production of "Tusitala" was at Hotel Del Monte grounds in Monterey and the second at the Forest Theater in Carmel. A review in the *Monterey Daily Cypress* said that "Lewis Josselyn overcame many obstacles as stage manager, the success of the masque in a large measure being due to his untiring work."[226]

Pomander Walk

Pomander Walk (1921)

In January 1917, Josselyn took a leave of absence from his position at the Western Drama Society to serve in the army during World War I.[227] Upon returning to civilian life, Josselyn rejoined the arts community of Carmel-by-the-Sea, resuming his involvement with the Forest Theater. In July 1921, he took on the role of theater photographer for the production of *Pomander Walk,* a historical comedy by the British playwright Louis N. Parker.[228]

This marked Josselyn's first major project at the Forest Theater since his return. The production, held on the evenings of July 2-4, 1921, drew large and enthusiastic audiences who gathered under the stars to enjoy the charming and nostalgic play set in a quaint 18th-century English village.[229] His wife, Jeanne, played

"Nanette," and his brothers, Winsor played Lt. John Sayle, and Talbert played Admiral Sir Peter Antrobus.[230]

Caesar and Cleopatra

Ruth Kuster as Cleopatra and harp player in 1922, photograph by Lewis Josselyn

In June 1922, Josselyn assisted Jack Williamson on managing the light switchboard during and after the rehearsals for the production of George Bernard Shaw's play *Caesar and Cleopatra* at Carmel's Forest Theater.[231]

The thirteenth season opened on July 6, 1922, Josselyn documented the production by photographing the actors and sets. Among his subjects were Ruth Kuster, who played *Cleopatra*, and writer Frederick R. Bechdolt, who portrayed Caesar. Ruth was the wife of Edward G. Kuster, who directed and performed in various plays at the Forest Theater.[232]

Josselyn's photographs captured the artistry of the production, From the Egyptian-themed sets, including a large replica of the Sphinx, were designed by artist Jo Mora. The set designs brought ancient Egypt to life on the Forest Theater's open-air stage.[233]

Hassan

In July 1923, Josselyn documented the Forest Theater's ambitious production of *Hassan: A Play in Five Acts* by James Elroy Flecker, which ran from July 2–4. The play tells the captivating tale of Hassan, a young man from Baghdad, and his journey to the legendary city of Samarkand in Central Asia. Rich in poetic imagery and mystical themes, *Hassan* offered an exotic and imaginative narrative that challenged the performers and designers to transport audiences to a faraway world.[234]

Josselyn's theory on stage lighting offered a thoughtful and artistic solution to the inherent challenges of outdoor theater, where the elements of light and shadow could be both a blessing and a limitation.

He emphasized that lighting should never be an isolated component but rather an integral part of the production's overall vision. Josselyn believed that lighting must serve the narrative and the director's concept, saying, *"To make your lighting a part of the whole scheme of things—to subordinate it to the producer's general idea, never to let it detract from the spoken line nor to descend to a trick effect just because it's a good trick effect just because it's a good trick. Light is really, you might say, the medium to which a production swims—but you must never forget the production in the medium."* This philosophy underscored his rejection of gimmickry or showy techniques that could distract from the performance. Instead, he championed the idea of lighting as a supportive and seamless element that enhances the mood, tone, and emotions of a scene."[235]

Inchling

Walter Gundelfinger in the play "Inchling," and the Butterfly and an Inchworm (1922), photos by Lewis Josselyn

Josselyn's next project occurred from August 18 to 19, 1922, when he handled the photography and collaborated once again with Jack Williamson, who served as the lighting artist, for Ira Mallory Remsen's three-act children's fantasy play Inchling. The play tells the story of Inchling and his quest to gain wings. Directed by Blanche Tolmie, the production featured nearly every child living in Carmel, each playing a "creature of the forest." The musical accompaniment for the dance performances was provided by Edward G. Kuster on cello and Jeanne Burton on piano.[236]

Josselyn played a key role to capture the sets, actors, and various scenes in the play, including Walter Gundelfinger as the First Robin, and Walter Flanders played the character Inchling, an inchworm. Josselyn's brothers, Talbert and Winsor, also participated in the production at the Forest Theater. Josselyn's mother helped with the wardrobe.[237][238] The play was the most popular children's play ever performed at the Forest Theater.[239]

Mr. Bunt

Set designers: Talbert and Winsor Josselyn, Brice
Monahan, Philip Wilson, and Rem Remsen, with
Phyllis Blake and Charlie Van Riper on set. Photos taken
by Lewis Josselyn in 1924.

In July 1924, Josselyn oversaw the stage lighting and photography for Ira Remsen's three-act children's fantasy play *Mr. Bunt*, which premiered at the Forest Theater from July 2 to July 5, 1924.[240]

Josselyn was able to photograph various scenes in the play. In the circus act, Phyllis Blake played Lu and Charles King Van Riper played Jim. Josselyn's brothers Talbert and Winsor Josselyn helped with set design and acted in the play.[241] Winsor played the Owl who held classes in silence. Talbert was the Milkman depositing his wares in milk-shrines.[242]

The play won a $100 (equivalent to $1,778 in 2023) award for the best original play submitted in the annual play contest held by the Forest Theater Society. It was the first time a play was presented at the Forest Theater with its own music composed for it and directed by the composer Frederick Preston Search with his own orchestra.

Romeo and Juliet

The set of Romeo and Juliet, with Herbert Heron as Romeo. Photographs taken in 1927 by Lewis Josselyn.

In the summer of 1927, Josselyn documented the Forest Theater's production of *Romeo and Juliet*, held on July 29–30. This outdoor event was a highlight of the season, showcasing the theater's commitment to bringing timeless classics to life. Herbert Heron took on the role of Romeo, while Jadwiga Noskowiak portrayed Juliet.[243] [244]

Josselyn's connection with Heron extended beyond *Romeo and Juliet*. He also photographed his acclaimed portrayal of *Hamlet* in 1926.

Heron's influence on Carmel's cultural life was profound. As the founder of the Forest Theater in 1910, he established the venue as a cornerstone of the community's artistic identity. Beyond his work as an actor and producer, Heron served two terms as Carmel's mayor during the 1920s, advocating for policies that supported the town's creative and cultural pursuits.[245]

Carmel Arts and Crafts Theater

While the Forest Theater served well as an outdoor venue during the summer, the village needed an indoor space for year-round performances. On March 16, 1922, Mary E. Hand, president of the Carmel Arts and Crafts Club, collaborated with playwright John Northern Hilliard to establish the Carmel Arts and Crafts Theater, where the local club could stage their own productions.

On October 27 and 28, 1922, Lewis Josselyn collaborated with Edward G. Kuster on the lighting for three one-act plays at the Carmel Arts and Crafts Theater: George Bernard Shaw's *The Dark Lady*, *A Night at an Inn*, and *The Rented Ranch*.[246]

The Dark Lady (1922) photo by Lewis Josselyn

The Arts and Crafts Theater's formal opening took place on November 28-29, 1922, featuring two plays—*The Thrice Promised Bride* and *The Queen's Enemies*—produced and directed by Hilliard.[247]

On December 8-9, 1922, Josselyn handled the lighting with Kuster for the three-act comedy *Cranford* and the one-act comedy *Spreading the News*, at the Arts and Crafts Little Theater.[248] [249]

On March 2-3, 1923, Josselyn was again in charge of lighting, this time for the play *Those Who Served*, designed and directed by Herbert Heron.[250]

The Man Who Married a Dumb Wife

The Man Who Married a Dumb Wife (1924), photo by Lewis Josselyn

Josselyn photographed the comedy in two-acts play *The Man Who Married a Dumb Wife* by Anatole France and directed by Herbert Heron, on May 30-31, 1924, at the Arts and Crafts Theater. He and his brother Talbert were listed on the producing staff. His brother Winsor played the lawyer character Master Adam Fumme.[251]

Talbert Josselyn, Phil Wilson, Winsor Josselyn. Photograph by Lewis Josselyn

On December 28, 1919, the *San Francisco Examiner* reported that the Forest Theater Society, the Western Drama Society, and Arts and Crafts would merge into a corporation under the state laws. The name of the new organization became "Forest Theater Society." Theodore M. Criley was instrumental in founding the new organization. James Hopper, F. R. Bechdolt, and John N. Hilliard were on a committee for play selections. Herbert Heron, M. DeNeale Morgan, Helen Parkes, Theodore M. Criley and Mary E. Hand, and others were on the board of directors. [252] [253]

The Bad Man

On January 15-16, 1926, Jo Mora
played Pancho Lopez, in the
three-act comedy, *The Bad Man*,
which opened at the Carmel
Arts and Crafts Theater, under
the direction of George M. Ball.
Josselyn photographed Mora's
portrayal in the theatrical
production.[254] [255] Talbert
Josselyn played Henry Smith,
the uncle.[256]

The play was performed again
in October 1928 at the Carmel
Playhouse, a venue that
underwent several name
changes over the years,
including the Abalone Theatre,

*Jo More in the play Bad Man (1928),
photo by Lewis Josselyn*

the Filmarte, and the Carmel Arts and Crafts Theater. It included
the original cast: Jo Mora, Byington Ford, Ernest Schweninger,
Talbert Josselyn, and Katherine Cooke.[257]

Woodblocks

In 1927, Josselyn used his own woodblocks to create posters for
productions at the Forest Theatre. Other artists like Louis
Legendre, Arthur Vachell, De Neale Morgan, and Perry
Newberry, used woodblocks to make posters for Forest Theater
plays, like *The Todd*, and *Alice in Wonderland*.[258]

Theater of the Golden Bough

Theater of the Golden Bough and auditorium (1924) photos by Lewis Joselyn

In 1925, Edward G. Kuster, a prominent figure in Carmel's arts community, designed and built his own indoor theater located within the Court of the Golden Bough on Ocean Avenue Carmel's main street. He called it the Theatre of the Golden Bough, which became known as an experimental theater and school.[259]

He borrowed the name from Roman mythology, where the Golden Bough refers to a branch with golden leaves, allowing the Trojan hero Aeneas to journey safely through the underworld. The theater's early photography was overseen by Josselyn. His photographs capture various features, including the auditorium with its 38 ft (12 m) with stage, as well as the Court of the Golden Bough. [260]

The theater included a summer drama school that included plays conducted by faculty and students. Josselyn was invited to the opening night where he photographed

Ellen Van Volkenburg in The Mother of Gregory (1924), photo by Lewi Josselyn

actress Ellen Van Volkenburg, who had the title-role in Maurice
Browne's play, *The Mother of Gregory*, which played June 6, 7, and
14, 1924 at the Theater of the Golden Bough.[261] [262] *The Princess Who
Wouldn't Say Die* was also produced by Maurice Browne and
played August 7 through 10, 1924.[263]

The plays were followed by a nine-week professional summer
drama school that became a place for theatrical education. In 1924,
Josselyn captured the portraits of the Carmel Summer School's
teaching staff, including notable figures such as Kuster, Maurice
Browne and Ellen Van Volkenburg, and others.[264]

*Summer school's teaching staff (1924), which
included Kuster, Maurice Browne and Ellen
Van Volkenburg, photo by Lewis Josselyn*

Browne and Van
Volkenburg, founders of
the Little Theatre
Movement, served as
directors of the school
during this time. Their
leadership brought an
innovative approach to
theater, emphasizing
intimate productions and
a focus on artistic
experimentation.[265]

Josselyn's portraits not only documented the individuals shaping
the school but also preserved a visual history of Carmel's artistic
community during this time.

Theater Fire

Theater of the Golden Bough Fire on May 19, 1935, photo by Lewis Josselyn

On May 19, 1935, Josselyn documented the aftermath of the devastating fire that destroyed the Theatre of the Golden Bough. The fire occurred just two days after Kuster had opened his production of *By Candlelight*, an adaptation of Siegfried Geyer's classic German comedy based on mistaken identity. Arson was suspected as the cause of the blaze.[266] [267]

Josselyn's photographs captured the charred remains of the theater, preserving a visual record of the destruction. The theater operation moved to the site of the former Carmel Arts and Crafts Club on Monte Verde Street, which later was renamed the Golden Bough Playhouse.[268]

Court of the Golden Bough

Court of the Golden Bough showing shops and entrance to Theater of the Golden Bough in the rear, ca. 1925 by Lewis Josselyn

Between the 1920s and 1930s, Josselyn's photographs documented the Tudor-style storefronts along the Court of the Golden Bough, a picturesque courtyard designed in the 1920s by Edward G. Kuster in front of his Theater of the Golden Bough. Kuster, a former lawyer-turned-theater director and arts advocate, envisioned the Court as part of a vibrant artistic center in Carmel.

Josselyn's images captured the architectural charm of the area, including notable establishments like the Carmel Weavers Studio (1922), Sade's (1924), and the Seven Arts Shop (1937). The Court of the Golden Bough quickly became a gathering place for artists, craftspeople, and visitors drawn to Carmel's creative and inspiring atmosphere.[269] [270]

Carmel Weaver's Studio

The Carmel Weaver's Studio and Ruth Kuster in front of the studio in the 1920s, photographed by Lewis Josselyn

In 1922, Kuster built the Carmel Weaver's Studio for his wife, Ruth, as a weaving shop in the Court of the Golden Bough, located in front of the Theatre of the Golden Bough on Ocean Avenue. Photographs of the studio appeared in an article published in the *Oakland Tribune* on November 19, 1922. while Josselyn was not credited for the images, they are well-documented as his work.[271] [272]

The following year, Kuster expanded the building to include a ticket booth for Ruth. Josselyn captured a photograph of her standing in front of the studio, with the signs for the Court of the Golden Bough and her handloom fabrics visible in the background.[273]

Today the building is known as the Cottage of Sweets, a favorite spot for tourists visiting Carmel.

Seven Arts Shop

Seven Arts Shop (1923), photograph by
Lewis Josselyn

The Seven Arts Shop was designed by Kuster and built in 1923, as a one-story, wood-frame Tudor Storybook-style shop, located on Ocean Avenue, next to the Carmel Weavers Studio in the Court of the Golden Bough in Carmel.[274]

Josselyn took the photographs of the building when it was known as "The Seven Arts" book and art store for Helena Conger and Herbert Heron. The building later served as a reding room for the Christian Science organization and then became the Robert Talbot Tie shop.[275]

The building has been recognized as a significant commercial property in the Carmel's *Downtown Historic District Property Survey* and was officially recorded with the Department of Parks and Recreation on January 23, 2002.[276] Today, it is one of the many retail shops that occupy Ocean Avenue.

Sade's

Sade's and the Carmel Weavers Studio, photo by Lewis Josselyn

In May 1924, novelist Harry Leon Wilson built a two-story Tudor-style building for his wife, Helen Wilson, who operated a floor flower shop on the ground floor and a dress shop upstairs. The building, located in the Court of the Golden Bough, was situated next to Carmel Weavers Studio and the Seven Arts Shop. Helen sold flowers and garden design services.[277]

Florist Now

Helen Wilson, wife of Harry Wilson, the author, has opened a flower shop at Carmel. In addition to selling blossoms she designs gardens.
—Photo by Lewis Josselyn.

In 1925, Josselyn took a photograph of the building when it was called The Bloomin' Basement.[278] The first floor became Sade's, a popular Bohemian bar and restaurant. Helen Wilson later moved the flower shop to the Amelia Gates Building a block away.[279]

1924 Florist Now newspaper clipping.

Other Actors

Other actors Josselyn photographed include:

- John Gribner (1915)[280]

- John Northern Hillard (1916) [281]
- Thomas Fisher (1923)[282]
- Ethel Turner (1924)[283]
- Richard Criley (1926) [284]
- Morris Wild (1926) [285]
- William T. Kibbler (1927)[286]

List of Plays

Josselyn did the photography for the following plays, which can be found at the Harrison Memorial Library or at the California Revealed websites.[287]

- The First Poet (1915)
- A Midsummer Night's Dream (1916)
- Tusitala (1916)
- A Lodging for the Night (1916)
- Saint Ives (1916)
- The Piper (1916)
- Yolanda of Cyprus (1916)
- A Thousand Years Ago (1917)
- Tents of the Arabs (1920)
- Snow White and the Seven Dwarfs (1920)
- The Golden Doom (1920)
- Yellow Jacket (1920)
- Countess Cathleen (1921)
- Pomander Walk (1921)
- A Night at an Inn (1922)
- Cathleen in Houlihan (1922)
- Caesar and Cleopatra (1922)
- King Henry IV (1922)
- Workhorse (1922)
- High Justice (1923)
- Twelfth Night (1923)
- Kismet (1923)
- Hassan (1923)
- The Cradle (1923)
- Quality Street (1924)
- Shore Acres (1924)
- The Man Who Married a Dumb (1924)
- Iphigenia in Taurus (1925)
- Hamlet (1926)
- Arms and the Man (1926)
- Romeo and Juliet (1927)
- If I Were King (1927)
- In the Shadow of the Glen (1927)
- Pinocchio (1929)
- The Romancers (1929)
- Julius Caesar (1930)
- Salome (1932)

CHAPTER THREE
Jo Mora Collection

Jo Mora working on California Carte, (1927) by Josselyn

T he Jo Mora collection features photographs taken by Josselyn, documenting many of his artistic achievements of Jo Mora (1876-1947), a prominent artist, sculptor, and writer, during his time in the Monterey Peninsula.

The collection captures Mora's works from individual pieces in development to fully realized projects, like the Carmel Dairy murals. Josselyn began working with Mora In 1921, who was a family friend and shared a passion for the arts as well as the creative community of Carmel during the 20th century.[288]

Pebble Beach Studio

The Jo Mora collection is a significant collection of wide-angle photographs and negatives, taken by Josselyn, capturing Mora within his studio in Pebble Beach, highlighting many of his creations, spanning from the mid-1920s to the mid-1940s.[289]

Jo Mora with "The Poppy Nymph" (1916) by Josselyn

In Mary Murray's book *Jo Mora: Artist and Writer*, several photographs by Josselyn are featured. These include Mora with his sculpture *The Poppy Nymph* (1916), Mora alongside *The Doughboy* in his studio (1920), Mora at Carmel Mission with the Junípero Serra cenotaph (1924), the installation of the Junípero Serra statue (1926), Mora inspecting the installation of the El Paseo statue in the courtyard of the El Paseo Building (1928), and Mora in his studio (1929).[290]

The book *The Life and Times of Jo Mora: Iconic Artist of the American West* features many descriptions and photographs by Josselyn. Included in this book is Mora's 24-inch model of the California Diamond Jubilee half dollar (1925), commemorating the 75th anniversary of California statehood. The book includes an initial plaster rendition of *The Cowboy* (1927), a Jo Mora *portrait* (1945), among other photographs. Many of these photographs are in the Barbara Josselyn Asa Collection.[291]

Doughboy

Winsor Josselyn, Jo Mora, Alice Josselyn, Jeanne Josselyn,
(1920) photo by Lewis Josselyn

In 1920, Lewis Josselyn captured a photograph of the
bronze Doughboy sculpture in the studio of its creator, Jo Mora.
The sculpture depicts a World War I infantryman, known as a
"Doughboy," who stands at attention in full uniform. The figure,
with his left foot forward, is adorned in the standard gear of a
soldier from the Great War: a steel helmet, leggings, a backpack,
and a pouch strapped across his chest.

The photograph not only highlights Mora's craftsmanship but also
captures a personal moment. In one of Josselyn's photos, Mora is
seen alongside the Josselyn family, which included Winsor, Alice,
and Jeanne.[292]

California Diamond Jubilee half dollar

Mora Designing a Jubilee half dollar Coin in Clay (1925) photo by Lewis Josselyn

In 1925, Josselyn photographed Mora designing a coin in clay that became the California Diamond Jubilee half dollar, a United States commemorative silver fifty-cent piece struck at the San Francisco Mint in 1925. It was issued to celebrate the 75th anniversary of California statehood.

The artworks created by Mora in his Pebble Beach Studio, many of which were featured in Josselyn's photographs, were displayed in an exhibit by the Monterey History and Art Association.[293]

Among the sculptures Josselyn photographed was "Fanning a Twister (1926)," a dynamic piece depicting a horse and rider. This particular sculpture was later included in the exhibit "Jo Mora: From Pencil to Publication," at the National Steinbeck Center in Monterey. The exhibit celebrated Mora's artistic journey, highlighting his transition from detailed pencil sketches to fully realized sculptures and other creative works.[294] [295]

Junípero Serra

Mora and his daughter at the father Serra shrine in Carmel Woods (1922) by Josselyn

Josselyn captured photographs of the Serra pilgrimage and Jo Mora's shrine, including the wooden statue of Father Junípero Serra, which was dedicated on July 22, 1922, during the opening day of the Carmel Woods subdivision. The event coincided with Serra Day; an official holiday proclaimed by the Carmel Town Trustees.[296] [297] That evening, the Carmel Mission hosted a performance *Serra,* a play by Garnet Holme at the Forest Theater.[298] [299]

The wooden statue of Junípero Serra was commissioned by Samuel F. B. Morse, president of the Del Monte Properties company. It stands within a tile-roofed wooden shrine, flanked by redwood benches at its base, at the entrance to Carmel Woods.[300]

Josselyn also captured photographs of significant events related to Junípero Serra, including the Carmel Mission Museum display in 1937, Serra's reinterment in 1943, and the Serra Cause Canonical Court proceedings at the Carmel Mission in 1948.[301]

Jo Mora in his studio showing Father Raymond Mestres the unfinished cenotaph of Junípero Serra (1922) photo by Lewis Josselyn

In 1922, Josselyn captured images of the Junípero Serra cenotaph (or sarcophagus) while it was still under construction in a workshop at the Carmel Mission. Jo Mora, who regarded the cenotaph as the pinnacle of his career, was captured in the images alongside Father Raymond Mestres, who had commissioned the work.[302]

Two years later, the completed bronze-and-travertine memorial cenotaph was unveiled at the Carmel Mission during the Serra Pilgrimage, commemorating the 140th anniversary of Father Junípero Serra's death. Josselyn documented Jo Mora posing next to the cenotaph in the small chapel on the south side of the mission.[303] [304]

Bronze cenotaph at the Carmel Mission (1924), photo by Josselyn

La Gitanita

Jo Mora in workshop with model for "La Gitanita" (1926) photo by Josselyn

In 1926, Josselyn took photos of Mora working on *La Gitanita* (The Little Gypsy) in his studio with a local model to pose for the project, *La Gitanita* with a Spanish dancer.[305]

Bronze Statue, 1926, photo by Lewis Josselyn

Byington Ford and his wife Marion, commissioned Mora to create three life-size portrait bronze figures of his daughters. Mora knew Byington from the relationship he had developed with Byington's father Tirey L. Ford, where Tirey authored a book titled, *Dawn and the Dons: The Romance of Monterey* with vignettes and sketches by Mora. The statues were made in Mora's large studio in Pebble Beach at the same time Mora was working on a clay statue of the Spanish dan cer *La Gitanita*, (The Little Gypsy).

Each portrait statue holds something unique and was positioned above a fountain at the Ford residence. Reflecting on the project, Mora remarked, "It was questioned who had more fun in the making, the children or I."[306]

Mora also created personalized drawings for close friends, including one for Josselyn. This particular piece was a heartfelt gift, symbolizing their friendship.

Drawing from Mora to Lewis Josselyn

Portolá Expedition Diorama

Portolá expedition diorama (1939), photographed by Lewis Josselyn; Josselyn and Mora working on the expedition sculptures.

From 1938 to 1939, Josselyn helped Mora in making and photographing his large *Portolá expedition* diorama, in Mora's workshop. The diorama portraying Gaspar de Portolá's discovery of San Francisco Bay was showcased at the 1939-1940 Golden Gate International Exposition and World's Fair on Treasure Island, which began on February 18, 1939. [307]

At a length of 100 ft (30 m), the diorama featured 64 sculptures of Spaniards and Native Americans, along with over 200 animals. It was a collaborative effort, with many of Josselyn's friends, including Ferdinand Burgdorff, assisting Mora in assembling and painting the figures.[308]

Carmel Dairy

Jo Mora's workshop with murals for the Carmel Dairy (1928)
photo by Lewis Josselyn

In 1943, Josselyn captured photographs of Jo Mora in his studio on three large murals commissioned for Earl F. Graff's Carmel Dairy. The building, also known as the Reardon Building—named after Thomas B. Reardon, a Carmel pioneer who settled in the area in 1906. The building was later recognized as an important commercial structure in the Downtown Historic District Property Survey *and* was officially recorded with the Department of Parks and Recreation on January 20, 2002.[309]

Mora's photographs depicted whimsical animal figures dressed as humans, a creative choice that brought charm and personality to his work. Many of these animal characters were modeled after or bore resemblances to actual residents of Carmel. Mora also designed the Carmel Dairy's menus, Christmas cards, and even milk bottles. A cow became the dairy's official logo.[310]

Other Photographs

Additional photographs by Josselyn related to Mora, were documented in Hiller's book *The Life and Times of Jo Mora: Iconic Artist of the American West*, include:

- Patty at Piano with a Mora designed lamp (1911)
- Robert Stranton and Jo Mora (1936)
- Jo Mora portrait (1945)

CHAPTER FOUR
Robinson Jeffers

Robinson Jeffers standing in the front doorway of Hawk Tower
(1925) by Lewis Josselyn

Robinson Jeffers became friends with Josselyn through his brother, Talbert, who was well-acquainted with many writers in Carmel. Josselyn took a series of photographs of the celebrated poet Jeffers, his family, and his iconic Tor House and Hawk Tower.[311] These photographs of Jeffers at Tor House are now part of the Robinson Jeffers Collection available at the Occidental College library.[312]

Hawk Tower

Josselyn captured multiple images of Jeffers including the 1925 cover photo of Jeffers posing in the doorway of his self-constructed Hawk Tower, dressed in black with his left hand resting on a stone.[313]

In 1981, Tom Leyde, editor of *The Californian,* wrote about the Pat Hathaway collection and Josselyn's photographs noting that one of the images featured Carmel poet Robinson Jeffers standing in front of his Hawk Tower in 1925.[314]

Robinson Jeffers standing in front of his Hawk Tower (1925) by Lewis Josselyn

Jeffers family passport photo (1929) by Josselyn

In another 1925 photograph shows Jeffers standing on the grass in front of Hawk Tower.[315] The 1925 portrait has been featured in various publications and is on display in the Tor House Foundation docent office. In 1980, Pat Hathaway published post cards of this same Jeffers photo for the Tor House Foundation.[316]

A 1929 passport photo of the four Jeffers can be found at the Harrison Library Park Branch and is reproduced in the booklet *Robinson Jeffers, Poet, 1887-1987 A Centennial Exhibition.*[317]

Tor House and Hawk Tower on Scenic Road, by Lewis Josselyn

Josselyn provided a photograph of Jeffers for inclusion in the book *Robinson Jeffers and the Sea* (1936) by Melba Berry Bennett. [318] [319]

Other Prominent People

Lewis Josselyn took numerous portrait photographs of prominent people in the Carmel and Monterey area, including artists Jo Mora, William Ritschel, and real estate developer Frank Devendorf. His portraits of these influential individuals and the bohemian lifestyle, document the vibrant artistic and cultural community during its formative years.

Josselyn's connections with local artists, actors, and other creatives allowed him to capture candid moments and significant events, highlighting the personalities that contributed to the region's rich artistic legacy.

Frederick R. Bechdolt

Bechdolt in Junípero Serra (1915), and photograph by Lewis Josselyn for The Saturday Evening Post (1941)

Josselyn took photographs of various people in Carmel, including western writer Frederick R. Bechdolt, with whom he collaborated several times and both were members of the Abalone League. As a photojournalist, Josselyn worked with Bechdolt on stories that were published in *The Saturday Evening Post.* In 1936, Josselyn's photographs illustrated an article in the *Post* by Bechdolt titled "Stampede, 1936 Model," about the modern gold rush to the hills, northwest of Winnemucca, Nevada.[320]

In July 1922, Josselyn, Leo Gottfried, and John Northern Hilliard were often guests and Frederick Bechdolt's house or each other's homes, as they were good friends.[321]

In the November 15, 1941, issue of the Post, Josselyn's photographs were featured in Bechdolt's article titled, *Uncle Sam Goes Prospecting,* published in *The Saturday Evening Post,* documenting their journey through a mining county. Bechdolt and Josselyn traveled through the mining county to capture the images needed for the article.[322]

Frank Devendorf

Frank Devendorf (1925) photos by Lewis Josselyn

In 1925, Josselyn captured several notable photographs of James Franklin Devendorf (1856-1934), one of the key figures in the development of Carmel-by-the-Sea. These photographs, showcasing Devendorf in various poses, were featured prominently on the front cover of *The Carmelite*, a local publication, as well as in the influential book *Carmel: A History in Architecture*.[323]

Devendorf, an early Carmel real estate developer, founded the Carmel Development Company, which was instrumental in subdividing and developing the land that would become the picturesque village of Carmel. Devendorf's legacy in Carmel is honored through Devendorf Park, a small public space named in his memory.[324]

The photographs taken by Josselyn not only document the man himself but also provide a visual connection to the era of Carmel's growth.

William Frederic Ritschel

Ritschel and one of his marine paintings (1925) photo by Lewis Josselyn

Josselyn photographed renowned marine painter William Frederic Ritschel (1864-1949) in his studio located in the Carmel Highlands. Ritschel, celebrated for his dramatic seascapes and mastery of marine themes, was a prominent figure in Carmel's thriving art community. He actively exhibited at the Carmel Arts and Crafts Club between 1913 and 1924 and remained an influential member of the Carmel Art Association for over two decades, showcasing his work alongside other leading artists of the era.[325]

One of Josselyn's notable photographs captures Ritschel standing beside one of his evocative marine paintings. The photograph was featured in Daisy Bostick's 1925 book, *Carmel at Work and Play*, a publication that documented the artistic and cultural vibrancy of Carmel-by-the-Sea. It also included an insert showcasing Ritschel's stone castle in the Carmel Highlands.[326]

August Englund

August Englund, Carmel policeman (1920s) photo by Lewis Josselyn

In the 1920s, Josselyn captured several significant photographs of August "Gus" Englund (1868–1935), who first served as Monterey's chief of police before being appointed Carmel's first police chief. Englund's legacy is deeply intertwined with the early history of Monterey County and Carmel-by-the-Sea, where he played a pivotal role in shaping the Carmel's law enforcement.[327]

One of the most memorable aspects of Englund's tenure was his partnership with "Black Betsy," a sturdy horse that he used for patrolling the unpaved streets of Carmel. Black Betsy became an iconic part of Englund's persona, often seen accompanying him as he made his rounds to ensure the community's safety.[328]

Josselyn's photographs of Englund and Black Betsy not only document the early days of Carmel's law enforcement but also capture the essence of a simpler time when a dedicated police chief and his loyal horse were at the heart of the community.

Charles King Van Riper

Charles King Van Riper in 1924, photo by Lewis Josselyn

Charles King Van Riper (1891-1964) was an accomplished American writer and playwright whose work gained national attention through his short stories published in widely circulated magazines. In addition to his literary achievements, Van Riper played a key role in the cultural life of Carmel-by-the-Sea as the founder of the Abalone League.[329]

In 1924, Lewis Josselyn captured a photograph of Van Riper during a performance of *Mr. Bunt*, a play by Ira Remsen. Van Riper portrayed Jim, a circus clown, in what became one of his most memorable roles. [330] The *Morning Press* reviewer Michael J. Phillips praised Van Riper's performance, noting that he "showed a great deal of acting ability" and brought depth and humanity to the character. Phillips highlighted Van Riper's skill in portraying Jim as "a faulty but likeable human being," transforming the clown from a mere theatrical figure into a multidimensional, relatable person."[331]

Ferdinand Burgdorff

Ferdinand Burgdorff (1930, by Lewis Josselyn

Josselyn captured a compelling photo of Ferdinand
Burgdorff (1881–1975) at work in his Carmel studio. In the 1930s,
Josselyn became acquainted with Burgdorff while assisting Jo
Mora in the creation of the large Portolá expedition mural, a
significant piece that commemorates the historic 1769 discovery of
San Francisco.[332]

Burgdorff gained national acclaim for his mastery as a landscape
painter, particularly his vivid depictions of the Monterey
Peninsula, Yosemite, and the desert Southwest.[333]

The 1930 Josselyn's photograph of Burgdorff at his easel offers a
glimpse into the creative process of an artist whose work helped
define the visual identity of the region.[334]

Thomas Vincent Cator

Thomas Cator at the piano (1915) photo by Lewis
Josselyn

Thomas Vincent Cator was a talented American composer whose contributions to the cultural life of the town included a recital for the Carmel Arts and Crafts Society on August 28, 1915, where his compositions were warmly received by the audience.[335]

In 1922, Cator wrote the composition operetta for the play *Inchling,* written by Ira Mallory Remsen, which was an enchanting story of an inchworm's struggle to grow wings capturing the imaginations of young children and adults alike.[336] A highlight of the production was the performance of Cator's songs by Hulda von Reinecker, a celebrated soprano from San Francisco.

The photo of Cator, which appeared in the Arts and Crafts Club Scrapbook, was accompanied by newspaper clippings that documented the event, preserving the significance of Cator's contribution to Carmel's arts scene.[337]

Arthur Cyril

Arthur Cyril at Ocean Avenue (1925), photo by Lewis Josselyn

Josselyn took this photograph of actor and producer Arthur Cyril, a well-known figure Carmel-by-the-Sea. The image shows Cyril with his ornamental wolfhound, Lady Vodka, in front of the Carmel Investment Company on Ocean Avenue, housed in the historic Glassell Building.

This photograph was featured in Daisy F. Bostick's book, *Carmel at Work and Play*, accompanied by the caption: "A bit of Ocean Avenue. Arthur Cyril, prominent actor and producer, with his ornamental wolfhound, Lady Vodka, in front of Glassell Building."[338]

Other People

Other people Josselyn photographed include:

- Josephine Guilbert at her cottage (1916)[339]
- Harry Ashland Greene in front of Greene Mansion (n/d)[340]
- Theodore Criley (1920s)[341]

- Helen MacGowan Cooke-Wilson (1925) [342]
- Sam Powers (1925) [343]
- James Hopper (1925) [344]
- Gene Byrnes (1925) [345]
- Perry Newberry (1925)[346]
- Joseph W. Hand (1925)[347]

- Delos Curtis (1925) [348]
- John Catlin (1928) [349]
- Thomas Bickle (1928)[350]
- Harrison Johnston (1929)[351]
- Thorne and John Boke[352]

CHAPTER FIVE
Big Sur

Josselyn captured photographs of the Bixby Creek Bridge

L ewis Josselyn is known for documenting the construction of
Big Sur's coastal highways and the iconic Bixby Creek Bridge
through his photography. His work provides a visual record, from
the 1920s to 1938, of the engineering feats and natural beauty that
shaped the area during the development of California's scenic
Highway 1. His historic photographs not only captured the
construction process but also the rugged landscapes of Big Sur,
highlighting the challenges faced during this ambitious project in
the 1930s.[353]

As early as September 1920, the *Carmel Pine Cone* reported that
Josselyn, along with artist George Seideneck, and others spent

several days at Charles W. Howland's camp near Idlewild, near Big Sur, hiking for twenty-five miles.[354]

In 1925, Josselyn began taking photographs of a redwood cabin constructed by local carpenter Sam Trotter on a cliff's edge in Big Sur for the Coastland Trails Club. Subsequently, in 1947, Bill and Lolly Fassett purchased the cabin and transformed it into the Nepenthe restaurant.[355]

In 1927, prior to the construction of the Bixby Creek Bridge and the completion of the highway, Josselyn captured images of travelers traversing the Old Coast Road to and from Big Sur. He photographed the Steel Bridge over Garrapata Creek, north of Big Sur.[356]

Post Homestead

Post homestead on Highway 1 in Big Sur (1930) photo by Josselyn

In September 1919, the three Josselyn boys were reported to have gone on a week-long hike along the coast near the Post Homestead.[357] In 1930, Josselyn returned to the area and photographed the Post homestead, located at the southern end of Big Sur. William

Brainard Post built his home on the site near the present-day campground.[358]

Josselyn documented the Machado-Tevis House, a building erected by two Portuguese whalers associated with the Point Lobos shore in in.[359] Additionally, Josselyn captured images of William Brainard Post's homestead and the Partington Homestead (1920) near Big Sur.[360]

Big Sur Coast Highway

Kyle Brown standing next to his Chevrolet truck on Highway One Big Sur (1926), photo by Lewis Josselyn

From 1928 to 1932, Josselyn photographed the San Quentin State Prison camp during the construction of the Big Sur Coast Highway,[361] documenting the building of California Highway 1 along the Big Sur coast. He continued capturing the highway's development from 1932 until its completion on November 27, 1932, creating a visual record of the landscape before and after the highway's opening.[362]

Other photographs taken by Josselyn of the Big Sur region includes Palo Colorado Canyon, California, Torres Canyon, the United States Forest Service ranger headquarters at Big Sur, Pico Blanco viewed from the coastline, the Little Sur River, and Slates Hot Springs.[363]

Bixby Creek Bridge

Bixby Creek Bridge under construction (1932) photo by Josselyn

Josselyn captured photographs of the Bixby Creek Bridge during its early construction in 1931 through 1932, and on November 23, 1932, during its dedication and opening to the public.[364] [365]

Josselyn published early photo postcards and calendars advertising the Monterey Bay Area, which included views of the Bixby Creek Bridge on the Big Sur coast, and crews building California Highway 1. He recorded a 200 ft (61 m) tunnel that leads to Partington Cove and the aerial tramway that hauled limestone onto small ships above Bixby Canyon.[366] [367]

Pfeiffer Ranch Resort

Pfeiffer's Ranch Resort in Big Sur Valley (1933), photo by Lewis Josselyn

In 1933, Josselyn photographed the Pfeiffer's Ranch Resort, which was the first resort in Big Sur. It operated from 1908 to 1935. John and Florene Pfeiffer managed the resort and hosted such as Robin Jeffers and his wife Una. John Pfeiffer donated a portion of this property to the state for use as the Pfeiffer Big Sur State Park.[368] [369]

Point Sur Lighthouse

In 1935, Josselyn photographed the Point Sur Lighthouse at Point Sur State Historic Park 24.6 miles (39.6 km) south of Monterey, California. The lighthouse was established in 1889.[370]

Point Sur Light, photo by Josselyn.

One example of the lighthouse can be found at the Monterey Museum of Art.[371]

Point Lobos

Point Lobos and Carmel Mission (1925) photo by Lewis Josselyn

As early as 1916, Josselyn began capturing the rugged beauty of Point Lobos, a coastal reserve in Monterey County. Through his lens, he documented iconic features such as the granite quarry, which overlooked the Point Lobos Cannery and Whalers Cove— once home to a Japanese fishing village.

Josselyn's camera also found the artists who gathered at Point Lobos, drawn by its dramatic cliffs, cypress groves, and sweeping ocean views. Among those he photographed were notable painters like John O'Shea, William Mitchell, William Watts, and Theodore Criley, whose works were inspired by the area's landscapes.

In the 1920s, Josselyn took a picture of *The View of Point Lobos,* which would later be featured in the *Carmel Pine Cone* on November 28, 1973. [372] Another significant image, *Carmel Mission Looking South Toward Point Lobos* (1925), captured the relationship between the historic mission and the rugged coastline beyond.[373]

CHAPTER SIX
Buildings

Paul Flanders Mansion "Outlands," (1925) by Josselyn

L ewis Josselyn photographed many landmarks and buildings
around the Monterey Peninsula and Carmel area due to his
involvement in the local arts and cultural scene. As a
photographer, he documented the changing artistic and
architectural landscape, capturing Carmel's expanding art
community. His strong connections with key cultural
organizations, like the Western Drama Society and the Carmel Art
Association, gave him access to important events, structures, and
artistic spaces. His photographs, especially of iconic buildings such
as Colton Hall, the Custom House, and Bixby Bridge, serve as a
historical record of the area's transformation into an artistic colony.

Lady Allen House

Lady Allen House (1915) photo by Lewis Josselyn

In 1915, Josselyn photographed the historic Old Lady Allen House, celebrated as California's first wood-frame structure and a prominent landmark in Monterey. Constructed in 1849 by Jane Bushton and Thomas Allen, the house occupies an essential place in the architectural and cultural history of California. It represented a significant shift from the region's traditional adobe construction to modern building practices, reflecting the changing landscape of mid-19th-century California.

The house was notable not only for its pioneering wood-frame design but also for its deep ties to the local community, earning it the affectionate moniker "Old Lady Allen House." Josselyn's photograph captures more than just the structure—it serves as a visual record of Monterey's evolution and important piece of California's history.[374] [375]

Monterey Pioneer Bakery

Monterey Pioneer Bakery in Monterey (1918) photo by Lewis Josselyn

In 1918, Josselyn photographed the historic Monterey Pioneer Bakery. Originally located on Alvarado Street, the bakery was later relocated to the intersection of Pearl and Munras Streets in Monterey.

The bakery was established by Honoré Escolle (1834-1895), a French immigrant who became a prominent businessman in Monterey. Escolle partnered with Dionisio Ruis to establish the bakery, combining European baking traditions with local ingredients to create goods that quickly became staples in the region.[376]

Josselyn's photograph of the Pioneer Bakery is a snapshot of Monterey's history during a time of transition and growth.

Murphy's Barn

Murphy's Barn (1919) photo by Lewis Josselyn

Murphy's Barn, recognized as the first house built in Carmel-by-the-Sea, holds a unique place in the history of the coastal community. Constructed in 1846 by Matthew M. Murphy, the structure initially served as both a residence and a barn.[377]

By the time Lewis Josselyn photographed Murphy's Barn in 1919, the building had already become a symbol of Carmel's early settlement and a tangible link to the town's origins. Josselyn's photograph captures the rustic charm and enduring craftsmanship of the structure.[378]

Kent Seavey, a noted architectural historian, included Josselyn's image in the 2002 registration form submitted to nominate Murphy's Barn as a historical landmark. The application highlighted the barn's significance as a surviving example of early California architecture and its association with the founding of Carmel.[379]

Stevenson House

Robert Louis Stevenson House (1920) by Lewis Josselyn

In 1920, Josselyn turned his lens to the Robert Louis Stevenson House in Monterey, California, capturing this historic site in both daylight and moonlight. Originally built in the 1830s as a two-story adobe structure, the building gained fame as a temporary residence of Scottish author Robert Louis Stevenson during his visit to Monterey in 1879.[380]

Josselyn's dual approach to photographing the house—capturing its charm in the of daylight and the mystery of moonlight—highlights his skill as a photographer. His images showcase the

Stevenson House by moonlight

adobe structure's enduring beauty, from its thick walls and tiled roof to the lush garden that surrounds it. Today, the Robert Louis Stevenson House is recognized as both a California Historical Landmark (#352) and a property listed on the National Register of Historic Places.[381]

Carmel Bathhouse

The Carmel Bathhouse above the beach at the foot of Ocean Avenue, (1920s) photo by Lewis Josselyn

Josselyn documented Carmel's first community bathhouse, a historic structure built in 1889 by Abbie Jane Hunter and Delos Goldsmith, who envisioned it as a welcoming facility for locals and visitors alike. Perched on a dune at the end of Ocean Avenue along Carmel Beach, the bathhouse became a landmark, providing changing rooms, rest areas, and fresh-water showers for those enjoying the beach and its cool coastal waters.

For forty years, the Carmel Bathhouse was a hub of social activity. In 1921, the City of Carmel purchased the property, recognizing its value to the community. However, by 1929, plans to clear the dune area led to its dismantling. Before this occurred, Josselyn took a series of photographs that captured the bathhouse in its final years.[382]

The bathhouse with views of Carmel Point and Point Lobos, photo by Lewis Josselyn

Fisherman's Wharf

Fish markets at Fisherman's' Wharf, Monterey (1929) photos by Lewis Josselyn

Josselyn captured photographs of Monterey's Fisherman's Wharf and surrounding buildings, offering a glimpse into the bustling maritime activity of the early 20th century. One notable image from 1920 features a coastal steamer near the Matteo Napoli Wholesale & Retail Fish Co., a hub of the local fishing industry at the time. Another photograph captures the Lewis Fish Market Selected Fresh Fish and Swains Fish Market on the West side of Fisherman's Wharf.

In 1929, Josselyn documented the F. E. Booth Cannery, located at Fisherman's Wharf, during a period of significant growth in the Monterey sardine industry. His photographs of the cannery illustrate the industrial scale of seafood processing and its role in shaping Monterey's identity

Matteo Napoli Wholesale & Retail Fish Co., Fisherman's' Wharf, Monterey (1920), photos by Lewis Josselyn

as a major fishing and canning center. These images reflect the evolution of Fisherman's Wharf from a small fishing dock to a thriving economic and cultural landmark.[383]

First Theater

California's First Theater (1920s) photo by Lewis Josselyn

Josselyn's photograph of the First Theater in California, located in Monterey, is a visual tribute to one of the state's most historically significant structures. Built in 1847 by Jack Swan, a sailor turned entrepreneur, the adobe and wood building originally served as a lodging house for sailors and travelers. Its transformation into a theater began when U.S. Army officers stationed in Monterey staged dramatic performances in the building during the California Gold Rush era.

The First Theater stands as the oldest theater in California, embodying the convergence of Mexican and American cultural influences during a pivotal time in the state's history. Constructed during California's transition from Mexican to American governance, the building reflects the architectural styles and materials of the era, with its adobe walls and redwood framing showcasing the practicality and resourcefulness of its builders.[384]

Hotel Del Monte

The reopening of the Hotel Del Monte in 1926, that became the
Naval Postgraduate School, photo by Lewis Josselyn

Josselyn photographed one of Monterey's most iconic landmarks, the Hotel Del Monte, through a series of photographs that captured both its grandeur and its moments of transformation.

On September 23, 1924, the Hotel Del Monte was ravaged by a devastating fire. Josselyn was on hand to photograph the aftermath, including an early morning image of Fire Chief Parker standing amidst the ruins just after sunrise.[385] [386] One of Josselyn's images of the fire appeared in *The Californian* on June 12, 1950.[387] Following a two-year reconstruction effort, the hotel was reopened on May 8, 1926, the hotel later became the Naval Postgraduate School.[388]

Fire at Hotel Del Monte on September 27, 1924, with Fire Chief, William Parker,
standing amid the ruins of the smoldering hotel, photos by Lewis Josselyn

De Yoe Building

De Yoe Building (1924) photo by Lewis Josselyn

In 1924, Josselyn captured the De Yoe Building, a Tudor-style architectural gem located on Dolores Street in Carmel-by-the-Sea. Designed and constructed by master builder M. J. Murphy, the building exemplifies the storybook charm that Murphy brought to many of Carmel's iconic structures. Its Tudor-style design, with steeply pitched gables, exposed wood framing, and intricate stonework, made it a standout feature of the town's eclectic architectural landscape.

The building served as the headquarters of the *Carmel Pine Cone*, the town's local newspaper, and housed the Denny-Watrous art gallery and theater, operated by Edward G. "Ted" Denny and Hazel Watrous.[389]

Josselyn's photograph of the De Yoe Building captured not just its architectural elegance but also its significance as a hub of artistic and cultural activity.

Amelia Gates Building

The Amelia Gates Building (1924) photo by Lewis Josselyn

In May 1924, Josselyn captured a series of photographs featuring the Amelia Gates Building, a significant structure in Carmel-by-the-Sea's artistic and cultural landscape.[390] This two-story, wood-framed building, constructed in 1924, reflects the architectural charm and community-oriented spirit that defined Carmel during the early 20th century. Designed by Amelia Gates, the building stands adjacent to the Seven Arts Shop and is situated at the west end of the Court of the Golden Bough, with the Theater of the Golden Bough as its backdrop.

Amelia Gates Building (1924) photograph by Lewis Josselyn

One notable subject of Josselyn's photographs is Helen Wilson, the proprietor of the "Bloomin' Basement," a flower shop located in the lower level of the Amelia Gates Building. Josselyn's images capture the physical details of the shop such as its charming displays and the inviting ambiance of the basement-level space.[391]

La Playa Hotel

La Playa Hotel during reconstruction (1925) by Josselyn

In 1925, Josselyn photographed the reconstruction of the historic La Playa Hotel, located on the southwest corner of El Camino Real and 8th Avenue in Carmel-by-the-Sea, after it was nearly destroyed by fire. He also captured images of the interior terrace dining rooms and fireplace in 1932.

In 1932, Josselyn returned to the La Playa Hotel to photograph its elegant interior spaces, including the terrace dining rooms and the grand fireplace.[392]

La Playa Hotel with a terrace dining room overlooking Carmel Bay

The building was recognized as a significant commercial building and was recorded with the California Register of Historical Resources on September 21, 2002.[393]

Mortimer Fleishhacker House

Fleishhacker House Side chairs (1925) by Josselyn

The Mortimer Fleishhacker House, often referred to as the Green
Gables Estate, is a historic and architecturally significant property
located at 329 Albion Avenue in Woodside, California. Built over
a span of several years, from 1911 to 1935, the estate features an
English manor-style house. The design of the house completed by
Charles Greene of the architectural firm Greene and Greene and
embodies elements of the Arts and Crafts movement, with an
emphasis on craftsmanship, natural materials, and traditional
design principles.

Josselyn's photographic work highlights the sunroom's hand-
carved furniture, which exemplified the fine craftsmanship and
artisanal quality of the furnishings throughout the estate. Among
the pieces captured in Josselyn's photographs was a beautifully
crafted card table, featuring a tooled-leather top, alongside four
side chairs and an armchair, each with intricately detailed,
pigmented leather seats.[394]

Highlands Inn

Highlands Inn (1925), photo by Lewis Josselyn

In 1925, Josselyn took this photograph of the Highlands Inn, a historic resort in Carmel Highlands, California This photograph was featured in Daisy F. Bostick's book, *Carmel at Work and Play*, accompanied by a caption: "From the windows of Carmel Highlands Inn you look down into the surf on the edge of a jade-green sea."[395]

The Highlands Inn, originally established in 1917, became renowned for its unique location perched above rugged cliffs overlooking the Pacific Ocean.

Operated today by Hyatt as the Hyatt Carmel Highlands, the inn continues to attract guests with its unparalleled vistas, fine dining, and proximity to iconic destinations such as Big Sur and Point Lobos State Natural Reserve.

Pine Inn

The Pine Inn, Ocean Avenue (1925), photo by Lewis Josselyn

Josselyn's photograph of the Pine Inn, one of Carmel-by-the-Sea's iconic landmarks, appeared in publications as early as 1925, capturing the charm and elegance of this historic hotel. [396] Originally known as the Hotel Carmelo, the Pine Inn represents a blend of Arts and Crafts, Tudor, and Spanish architectural styles. Established in 1889 by pioneer Santiago J. Duckworth, it was Carmel's first full-service hotel.

In 1904, Frank Devendorf, one of Carmel's founding developers, renamed the property the "Pine Inn." Recognized for its historical significance, the Pine Inn qualified for inclusion in *Carmel's Downtown Historic District Property Survey* and was officially listed on the California Register of Historical Resources on March 18, 2003. Today, the Pine Inn continues to operate as a full-service hotel, inviting guests to experience a living piece of Carmel's storied past.

D. L. James House

D. L. James at Carmel Highlands (1925), photo by Lewis Josselyn

Josselyn photographed the home of Daniel Lewis James, located in
Carmel Highlands, California, designed by architect Charles
Sumner Greene, a partner in the architectural firm Greene and
Greene. Perched on a bluff overlooking the Pacific Ocean, the
house was commissioned by James's father, who purchased the
property and envisioned a Mediterranean-style retreat.
Constructed from sandstone and granite, the residence
exemplifies the craftsmanship and attention to detail for which
Greene and Greene are celebrated.[397]

Daniel Lewis James, a noted American writer, grew up
surrounded by the beauty of this extraordinary home. Best known
for his novel *Famous All Over Town*, James brought to life the
struggles and triumphs of Mexican American communities in Los
Angeles during the mid-20th century. Published under the
pseudonym "Danny Santiago," the novel gained critical acclaim
for its authentic portrayal of cultural identity, social injustice, and
urban life.[398]

Sunset School

Sunset School (1926) photo by Lewis Josselyn

In February 1926, Josselyn photographed the Sunset School, which had played a central role in the community's educational development.[399] Originally constructed in 1903, the school stood as one of the first public institutions in Carmel.

In 1929, renowned Carmel builder M. J. Murphy was commissioned to design and construct two additional classrooms for the Sunset School, located at the northwest corner of Mission Street and 10th Avenue. Josselyn's photographs from 1926 document the school in its earlier form, capturing the original building and the newly added classrooms.

By 1931, the school had outgrown its original capacity, leading to the construction of a 718-seat auditorium designed to accommodate the growing student body and the cultural activities that were becoming integral to Carmel's identity.

Today, the Sunset School building—now called the Sunset Center—continues to serve the community as a performing arts center which features concerts, comedy, theatre, and dance.[400]

Seven Arts Building

Seven Arts Building (1927) photo by Lewis Josselyn

In 1927, Josselyn photographed the Seven Arts Building, a key architectural and cultural landmark in Carmel-by-the-Sea, which housed the Carmel Art Association's first formal gallery. The building is located at the corner of Ocean Avenue and Lincoln Street.

The Seven Arts Building was built in 1925 for Herbert Heron, housed a bookshop and printing press. The building was constructed using Thermotite fireproof concrete blocks, a durable and innovative material that was both practical and aesthetically pleasing.

In addition to serving as a gallery, the second floor also became a home to photographer Edward Weston's studio, where he worked between 1927 and 1937.[401]

Josselyn's photographs of the Seven Arts Building captured not only its architectural beauty but also the cultural significance of the space.

Seven Arts Courtyard

Seven Arts courtyard (1920s), photo by Lewis Josselyn

Later, Herbert Heron expanded his vision by adding a cluster of buildings around a charming courtyard next to the Seven Arts Building on Lincoln Street. This courtyard became a focal point for the arts and commerce, reflecting Heron's dedication to creating a space that blended functionality with Carmel's artistic sensibilities.[402]

These photographs offer a glimpse into the community's culture at the time, showcasing the shops that occupied the space—likely including art studios, bookstores, and boutique retailers that catered to Carmel's creative and intellectual residents. Josselyn's work immortalizes

Lincoln Street Building (1920s), photo by Lewis Josselyn

Heron's vision of a lively, interconnected artistic hub, preserving its significance in Carmel's history.

Harrison Memorial Library

Harrison Memorial Library (1928) photo by Lewis Josselyn

Harrison Memorial Library, located on Ocean Avenue in Carmel, was designed by architect Bernard Maybeck and built by master builder Michael J. Murphy in 1928. On August 11, 1928, Josselyn captured a striking photograph of the newly completed library, documenting the elegance and craftsmanship of the building.[403]

Today, the public library continues to serve as a vital resource for the community, preserving the legacy of Maybeck's design and Josselyn's photographic work. The Harrison Memorial Library Park Branch, located at Mission Street and 6th Avenue, houses a rich collection of manuscripts and photographs, including works by Lewis Josselyn. Many of these have been digitized and made accessible online through platforms such as the Internet Archive and California Revealed.

El Paseo Building

El Paseo Building and El Paseo sculpture (1928), photos by Lewis Josselyn

The El Paseo Building, a two-story Spanish Eclectic-style structure on Dolores Street and 7th Avenue in downtown Carmel, was built in 1928. That same year, Josselyn photographed the building along with installation of "The Greeting," a terracotta sculpture by Jo Mora located in the El Paseo courtyard of the building. The sculpture depicts a Californio man and a Señorita woman. Today, the courtyard serves as an outdoor dining area for the Little Napoli restaurant.[404] [405]

The building and sculpture, representative of Carmel's downtown historic district, and were recorded with the National Register of Historic Places in January 2002. The El Paseo sculpture is as an excellent example of the artistic and cultural contributions of Jo Mora to Carmel in the 1920s.[406]

Draper Leidig Building

Draper Leidig Building (1929) photo by Lewis Josselyn

The Draper Leidig Building is a two-story Spanish Colonial-style landmark constructed in 1929 and located on Dolores Street in downtown Carmel-by-the-Sea.

Josselyn's photograph, taken on May 26, 1929, captured the building in its early days, preserving its architectural details and setting within the town's evolving landscape.

Characterized by stucco exteriors, red-tiled roofs, and decorative wrought iron elements, the building reflects the influence of California's Spanish colonial heritage while embracing modern elements of the time.

At the time of Josselyn's photograph, the building hosted four retail shops, providing a space for local merchants to sell their goods and serve the community.[407]

The building has been recognized as an important commercial building in the city's *Downtown Conservation District Historic Property Survey,* and was nominated and submitted to the California Register of Historical Resources on May 22, 2002.[408]

Tuck Box

Sally's Tea Room (1928) photo by Lewis Josselyn

In 1926, architect Hugh Comstock, known for his distinctive Storybook-style buildings, designed a building on Dolores Street, located between Ocean and 7th Avenue in Carmel-by-the-Sea. The design reflected Comstock's unique approach to architecture, which drew inspiration from fairy tales and European cottages, using steeply pitched roofs, arched doorways, and textured stonework.

By the late 1920s, the building had become known as Sally's Tea Room, a gathering spot that offered locals and tourists a taste of tea and light refreshments in a fairytale setting.

Josselyn, drawn to capturing Carmel's distinct architecture and vibrant culture, photographed Sally's Tea Room in 1928, preserving its early look and inviting presence.

In the following years, the tearoom evolved into what is now known as the Tuck Box. Josselyn's 1928 photograph Sally's remains a window into the early years of this landmark.[409]

Colton Hall

Colton Hall (1929) photo by Lewis Josselyn

Colton Hall, located in Monterey, California, is one of the area's most historically significant buildings. Serving both as a government building and a museum, it holds an important place in California's history, particularly for its role in the state's early government and its connection to the founding of the state's constitution. Built between 1847 and 1850, Colton Hall originally housed the offices of the local government and became the site of the 1849 California Constitutional Convention. It was here that delegates met to draft the state constitution in the lead-up to California's admission to the United States.

Josselyn's photographs of Colton Hall capture the building at different points in time, providing a visual record of the structure itself including the municipal Rose Garden adjacent to Colton Hall.[410]

Recognizing its importance, Colton Hall was registered as a California Historical Landmark in 1934.[411] [412]

California Missions

Throughout his career, Lewis Josselyn developed a distinctive portfolio of photographs that captured the beauty, history, and significance of California's historic missions and landmarks. His photographic works, spanning several decades, document not only the architectural splendor of these sites but also the cultural and historical essence of California itself.

San Diego Mission

San Diego Mission (1909), photograph by Lewis Josselyn

One of Josselyn's early works was his 1909 photograph of the San Diego Mission in Mission Valley, also known as Mission Basilica San Diego de Alcalá, one of California's oldest and most historically significant missions. [413] This photograph captures the elegance of the mission's Spanish colonial architecture, set against the backdrop of the San Diego River in Mission Valley. The San Diego Mission, founded on July 16, 1769, is often considered the birthplace of European civilization in California. Josselyn's image brings attention to California before freeways.

Plaza Church in Los Angeles

Plaza Church Los Angeles (1915) photo by Lewis Josselyn

In 1915, Josselyn captured a series of photographs of the Plaza Church in Los Angeles, formally known as La Iglesia de Nuestra Señora la Reina de los Ángeles (The Church of Our Lady Queen of the Angels). This historic Catholic church, founded in 1814, is one of the oldest religious institutions in the city and a central figure in the history of early Los Angeles. Located near the heart of the city's original settlement, El Pueblo de Los Ángeles, the church stands as a testament to the region's Spanish and Mexican heritage.

Josselyn's photographs highlight the church's Spanish Colonial Revival architecture, including its adobe walls, arched doorways, and distinctive bell tower, which is topped by a cross. His images not only emphasize the structure's elegant simplicity but also document its location alongside the Brunswig Drug Company, a prominent commercial building of the era, reflecting the juxtaposition of old and new in the rapidly modernizing city.[414]

Mission San Francisco Solano

Mission San Francisco Solano Sonoma California (1920), photograph by Lewis Josselyn

In 1920, Josselyn photographed Mission San Francisco Solano, located in Sonoma, California, capturing a pivotal piece of California's rich mission history. This mission, founded in 1823 by Father José Altimira, holds the distinction of being the northernmost and last of the 21 Spanish missions established in California. Unlike earlier missions built under Spanish rule, Mission San Francisco Solano was constructed during the Mexican era, following Mexico's independence from Spain in 1821.

Josselyn's photograph highlighted the mission's unique architectural features, including its simple adobe construction, whitewashed walls, and red-tiled roof.[415]

Mission San Antonio de Padua

Mission San Antonio (1928), photograph by Lewis Josselyn

Josselyn captured several images of Mission San Antonio de Padua in 1928, a mission founded on July 14, 1771, in the rugged hills of present-day Monterey County, California.

His photograph of this isolated and less-visited mission conveys the tranquility of its remote location and its distinctive, well-preserved architecture. The mission's original adobe walls and the expansive surrounding landscape are carefully documented in Josselyn's work, emphasizing the mission's connection to the natural environment.[416]

San Carlos Cathedral in Monterey

San Carlos Cathedral in Monterey, photo by Lewis Josselyn

In 1929, Josselyn photographed the historic San Carlos Cathedreal, officially known as the Cathedral of San Carlos Borromeo in Monterey. This cathedral, the oldest stone building in California and the oldest continuously functioning parish in the state, holds deep historical and spiritual significance as the first cathedral in California.

San Carlos Cathedral

Josselyn's photographs from this period offer a detailed view of the cathedral's architecture and its surrounding features. One notable focus of these images is the brick wall that enclosed the property at the time, emphasizing the structure's traditional design and its role in defining the sacred space.[417]

Carmel Mission

Carmel Mission photographs (1930s) by Lewis Josselyn

Josselyn collaborated closely with Harry Downie, the renowned restorer of the Carmel Mission, to document its restoration efforts, including the intricate work on the wooden ceiling arches after the significant renovation in 1936. Josselyn's photography preserves the craftsmanship and architectural transformation during this time.[418] [419]

Josselyn's collection also includes rare images from the earlier 1919 restoration, providing a detailed visual record of the Mission's evolving restoration history. These photographs feature the chapel's interior before and during the installation of the new wooden ceiling arches, with scaffolding intricately arranged to support the painstaking process.[420]

Additional photographs from Josselyn's collection portrays the cell where Father Junípero Serra, the Mission's founder, died—a space steeped in historical and spiritual significance. [421] Other exterior shots capture the Mission's timeless beauty, showing its stone facade, bell tower, and surrounding landscape.[422] One photograph looks south through the Mission gate, framing the Mission's architecture against the surrounding landscape. [423]

World War Memorial Arch

On Armistice Day, in front of the World War I Memorial Arch (1921) and
Fire Truck No. 4 in front of arch (1932), photos by Lewis Josselyn

Josselyn captured early images related to the dedication and laying of the cornerstone for the World War I Memorial Arch on Armistice Day, November 11, 1921.[424]

The World War I Memorial Arch, located on Ocean Avenue, soon became an enduring symbol of Carmel's history and was a recurring feature in Josselyn's later works. In 1932, he photographed Carmel Fire Truck No. 3 parked in front of the arch, blending the iconic backdrop with the town's modern firefighting equipment, creating a powerful contrast between tradition and progress.[425]

In 1934, Josselyn expanded his documentation of the town's infrastructure by photographing the Carmel Fire Station, along with its fleet of fire engines and a police motorcycle. These images provide a detailed record of the vehicles and equipment used during this era, showcasing the evolving capabilities of Carmel's emergency services. Together, Josselyn's photographs not only chronicle significant events and landmarks but also reflect the growth and development of a close-knit coastal community.

Jarvis House

Charles F. Jarvis, photo by Lewis Josselyn

Josselyn photographed a quaint house designed by his friend architect Leo E. Gottfried, for Mrs. Charles F. Jarvis. This small home reflects the charm and craftsmanship of Carmel's architectural style in the early 20th century.

Today, Josselyn's photograph of the Jarvis House is housed in the online collection of the Art, Design & Architecture Museum, providing the public with access to a piece of Carmel's history and offering insight into the styles and stories that shaped the community.[426]

Paul Flanders Mansion

Paul Flanders "Outlands," (1925) photo by Lewis Josselyn

In 1926, Josselyn undertook the detailed documentation of the architecture of the *Outlands*, an estate located within the "Eighty Acres" in Carmel-by-the-Sea. The project was part of the Paul Flanders Mansion Historic American Buildings Survey (HABS), a federal initiative established to create a permanent archival record of historically significant structures across the United States. His work provided a contribution to preserving the unique architectural heritage of Monterey County. These photographs gained recognition for their historical and architectural significance, eventually becoming part of Monterey County's National Register of Historic Places listings. They also hold a prominent place in the National Park Service's digital assets gallery.[427]

Flanders Mansion (1925) photograph by Lewis Josselyn

The city of Carmel enlisted historian Kent Seavey to carry out the HABS to document the Flanders Mansion located at 25800 Hatton Road. The survey incorporated photographs by Josselyn, captured shortly after the mansion's construction. These images are important as they predate any alterations made to the site.[428]

T. J. Brennan House

The T. J. Brennan House on Scenic Road (1936) photo by Lewis Josselyn

Dr. T. J. Brennan, from Baguio, Philippines, built a distinctive two-story Tudor-style home in 1936 featuring a stone veneer exterior, located on 26097 Scenic Road and Martin Way on Carmel Point, just beyond the Carmel city limits.[429]

Lewis Josselyn captured the house in a series of photographs commissioned by its then owner, Ernest Bixler. These images document the home's unique architectural features, such as its steeply pitched gabled roof, stone facade, and decorative woodwork.[430]

Dr. T. J. Brennan House on Scenic Road (1936) photo by Lewis Josselyn

Over the years, the T. J. Brennan House has undergone renovations aimed at preserving its historic character while modernizing its amenities. Careful restoration efforts have ensured the home remains true to its original 1930s design, retaining the charm and craftsmanship that made it a standout structure in Josselyn's photographs.[431]

Gate House

Gate House, photo taken by Lewis Josselyn in the 1940s

The Gate House, situated on Isabella Street on Carmel Point, is a distinctive structure that exemplifies the area's historic charm and architectural heritage. Photographed by Josselyn in the 1940s, the Gate House was an integral part of the Charles King Van Riper estate, which spanned four expansive lots and included a caretaker's cottage. Josselyn knew Van Riper in 1924 when they were both involved with the performance of the play *Mr. Bunt* at the Forest Theater.[432]

The cottage itself is a striking example of local craftsmanship, featuring a roof with extended rounded eaves. Its exterior walls, constructed from native Carmel stone, blend with the natural surroundings.[433]

Other Buildings

Other buildings Josselyn photographed include:

- House of the Four Winds (no date)[434]
- Carmel Point House off Isabella (no date)[435]
- Edgemere Cottage (no date)[436]
- 8th Avenue House (no date)[437]
- Sherman Rose Adobe (1915)[438]
- Alvarado House (1916)[439]

- Sleepy Hollow House (1916)[440]
- Napoleon's Tomb, France (1918)[441]
- First Brick House (1920) [442]
- Produce Packing Shed (1920)[443]
- Monterey Block, San Francisco (1920)[444]
- Henry F. Dickinson House (ca. 1923)[445]
- Carmel Investment Company Building (1925)[446] [447] [448]
- Carmel Garage Ford showroom & Chevron Station (1925)[449]
- Edward Kuster's stone house[450]
- Fremont House (1929)[451]
- Hatton Ranch (1930s)[452]
- Carmelo Athletic and Social Club (1930)[453]
- View from rocks on coast of Pacific Grove (1930)[454]
- Custom House (1925, 1929, 1931)[455]
- Buildings on Lighthouse Avenue in Pacific Grove (1932)[456]
- Carmelite Monastery (1932)[457]
- Grace Deere Velie Metabolic Clinic (1934)[458]
- Bridgeport Court House, Mono County (1935)[459]

CHAPTER SEVEN
Later Years

Carmel Art Association gallery in the Seven Arts Building (1927)
photo by Lewis Josselyn

L ewis Josselyn remained active as a photographer in Carmel
and the surrounding area from the 1920s through the 1950s. In
April 1926, Josselyn conducted a photographic survey of
the Mojave Desert and Death Valley in the Southwestern United
States. He went again in May with playwright John Northern
Hilliard and others to live among and photograph the Hopi and
the Navajo peoples. Hilliard was planning a production of "Fire" a
play by Mary Austin.[460]

On June 6, 1926, Josselyn and wife returned to Carmel following an
auto tour through Arizona and Utah.[461]

Italian Hillside by George Seidenbeck (1927)
photo by Lewis Josselyn

Josselyn's images of contemporary Carmel paintings were often replicated in local and national publications. In 1927, his camera captured the painting *Italian Hillside* by George Joseph Seidenbeck, exhibited at the Carmel Art Association's formal opening on October 15, 1927, held at the organization's headquarters in Carmel. Other painters that exhibited were Theodore Criley, William Watts, and John O'Shea.[462] In 1933-34, he took photographs of the paintings that were exhibited by John O'Shea at the California Palace in the Legion of Honor in San Francisco.[463]

On December 14, 1928, the *Carmel Pine Cone* said: "His camera has caught Carmel's beauty spots. His brush has painted them. Forest Theater's official photographer."[464]

Before the Great Depression in 1929, Josselyn photographed portraits of early Carmel residents, like the wife of Charles Chapel Judson, who was the founder of the art department at the University of California, Berkeley.[465]

In December 1929, Lewis helped George E. Stone from Carmel Highlands, to photograph 200 of the statues on exhibit at the Legion of Honor in San Francisco. This was the largest exhibit at the Legion of Honor. The photographs were later used as slides for schools, art appreciation classes, and lectures.[466]

Monterey Cypress, Seventeen Mile Drive, oil painting by Lewis Josselyn

At the October 1931 Monterey County Fair, Josselyn exhibited two paintings—one in oil and another in watercolor, which were described as "both pleasing," by Eleanor Minturn James.[467]

In August 1934, the *Carmel Pine Cone* announced that Josselyn, along with friends, Jo Mora, Byington Ford, Lee Gottfried, Winsor Josselyn, M. J. Murphy, and others, had joined the Citizens Committee of Carmel, a group dedicated to preserving the law and order and preventing acts intended to disrupt the government by force.[468]

That same year, Josselyn shared a special Christmas sentiment, expressing, "If I could be in three places at once on these bright winter days to take pictures in this matchless region."[469]

Publications

Josselyn's photographs have been the subject in many articles across national and regional publications such as the *Sunset Magazine, The Christian Science Monitor, Carmel Pine Cone, The Saturday Evening Post,* and in material used for documenting the historic architecture for the Historic American Buildings Survey (HABS).[470]

In January 1925, Daisy Bostick published, *Carmel at Work and Play,* which highlights notable photographers from the Monterey Peninsula. According to Bostick "Beautiful photography of the kind which requires both the skill of the craftsman, and the soul of the artist is well represented in Carmel by the work of Lewis Josselyn, Louis S. Slevin, and Johan Hagemeyer." Bostick features many images by Josselyn, including captures of the Cypress Trees of seventeen-mile drive, the Pine Inn, Carmel Highlands, the Forest Theater stage, developer Frank Devendorf, Carmel mayor Perry Newberry, and the Carmel Investment Company.[471]

A Monterey Cypress (1927), photo by Lewis Josselyn

In 1927, Josselyn's photographs started to appear in magazines like the *California Southland,* where a picture of a *Monterey Cypress* appeared.[472]

The *Christian Science Monitor* of June 4, 1932, about wildflowers written by Lester Rowntree had a reproduction of a photograph, "Arched Gate in Rock Garden on Pacific Coast," by in Josselyn.[473]

Lester Rowntree

Aesculus Californica by Lewis Josselyn

Between 1930 and 1955, Josselyn collaborated with botanist and horticulturist Lester Rowntree of Carmel Highlands, to photograph California native plants, including the *Chrysolepis chrysophylla*, for *The National Horticultural Magazine.*[474] [475]

Oenothera Ovata (1935), photo by Lewis Josselyn

In May 1930, Josselyn's nature and botanical photography were featured in two articles by Mrs. Lester Rowntree published in *California's Natural Costal Flower Gardens* and in *Sunset Magazine*.[476]

For the May 1930 edition of *Sunset Magazine*, Lester Rowntree wrote an article "Homes in the Highlands," with photographs by Lewis Josselyn. Photographs include images of a bird's-eye view, doorways, stone fireplaces, and wildflowers of several Carmel Highlands homes.[477]

In 1935, Josselyn contributed photographs for the *A Textbook of General Botany*, by Gilbert M. Smith. Photographs included Sea palms and bull kelp.[478]

In 1937, Josselyn traveled to Pasadena to spend Christmas with his family.

Conde McCullough Memorial Bridge Coos Bay Oregon (1936), photo by Lewis Josselyn

In 1936, Josselyn photographed the Conde McCullough Memorial Bridge that spans the Coos Bay on U.S. Route 101 near North Bend, Oregon. He also captured photographs of the Pendleton Round-Up in September 1929, a rodeo event held in in Pendleton, Oregon, known for its vibrant celebration of Native American culture and Western traditions.[479]

In October 1940, Josselyn prepared for the 10th annual turkey shoot as members of the Monterey Peninsula American Legion assembled portable buildings and booths at the shooting ranges along the Monterey-Salinas Highway (State Route 68), three miles from Monterey.[480]

During World War II, Josselyn registered with the U.S. Government draft department in 1942 at the Officer of the Post Quartermaster at Ford Ord in Monterey, California.[481]

The 1950 U.S. Census shows the family still living on Santa Rita Street in Carmel, with Lewis, now 67, listed as photographer, and Jeanne, 54.

Josselyn at the American Legion Post 512, at age 80

One of the final photographs of Josselyn was taken on May 20, 1963, during a banquet dinner attended by members of the Manzanita Club, a pioneer men's social group associated with the American Legion Post 512. Others at the event were with Fred Leidig, Lee Gottfried, Barnet J. Segal, and others.[482]

In 2009, Michael Kenneth Hemp, wrote the book *Cannery Row,* chronicling the history of Cannery Row that featured photographs by Josselyn. These images included scenes from:

- Point Lobos Canning Company (1916)
- Abalone divers and shells (1916)
- Monterey Bay storm (1919)
- Hotel Del Monte fire (1924)
- Lighthouse Avenue in Pacific Grove (1932)[483]
- Grove Theatre in Pacific Grove (1936)[484]

Equipment and techniques

Josselyn employed 5 inches (130 mm) x 7 inches (180 mm) large-format glass plate negatives for photographing his images. Printing these negatives required a large-format enlarger. As a copyright notice, he often used a hand-operated embossing technique along the bottom edge of his photographs, creating a raised imprint that read "L. Josselyn." One of the earliest photographs featuring this stamp was from the 1915 play *The First Poet*. He also used an ink stamp on the back of printed photographs. A typical stamp would say "Photograph by Lewis Josselyn." Photograph locations were sometimes noted on back in pencil.[485]

Josselyn's photography style was characterized by pictorialism: a soft-focus and use of natural light to evoke mood and atmosphere. One of Josselyn's contributions to photography was his experimentation with "Genuine Moonlight Photography," to capture his subjects like Point Lobos and the Stevenson house. [486]

Death

Josselyn remained active in photography and community life in Carmel until his death on March 14, 1964, at the age of 81. He died at his home at Santa Rita Street & 7th Avenue, Carmel from complications following a stroke he suffered two weeks earlier. A private service was held at the Little Chapel-by-the-Sea in Pacific Grove, lead by the Monterey American Legion Post No. 41.[487] [488] He and his wife are both buried together and share the same headstone at the Golden Gate National Cemetery in San Bruno, California.[489]

Legacy

After Josselyn's death, his sister-in-law, Florence Josselyn, showcased his 1920s and 1930s photographs at the historic Casa Serrano in Monterey in 1965.[490] She also organized a formal retrospective of his work at the Marjorie Evans Gallery in the Sunset Center in March 1973. Frank H. Riley, Director of

Community and Cultural Activities, wrote in the *Carmel Valley Outlook*: "I think you will find our new exhibit in the Marjorie Evans Gallery one of fun as well as of interest. We call it "The Carmel of Lewis Josselyn." It is made up of numberless photos taken by Lew Josselyn while Carmel was growing up." The exhibit included images of the Abalone League, the Monterey oil fire, the coastline, and the village.[491]

In 1968, Elver A. Barker published a painting titled "Cypress by the Sea," made from a photograph taken by Lewis Josselyn. Permission was given by Florence Josselyn.[492]

Josselyn's widow, Jeanne, tried to find a home for her husband's photographs, however, most libraries and institution did not have space or a way to print the glass negatives.[493] In November 1970, Jeanne gave about 3,000 original glass plates and film negatives, sized at 5 inches (130 mm) x 7 inches (180 mm), as well as original prints and his photographic equipment to Pat Hathaway, a photo archivist for one dollar.[494] The negatives span the period from 1914 to 1940. Josselyn's collection was the beginning of Hathaway's career as a photo archivist.[495]

Hathaway organized the Josselyn collection and assigned catalog numbers, dates, names, and locations to each photograph.[496] He actively promoted and exhibited Josselyn's photographs throughout the 1970s and 1980s. On March 10, 1973, Hathaway held an exhibition of his historical photographs at the Pacific Grove Art Center.[497] In 1981, Hathaway held another exhibit at the same location.[498]

Collections

Since Hathaway's death in 2021, Josselyn's inventory of glass plates and film negatives have been archived at the Monterey County

Historical Society in Salinas, California. They are open to the public and can be reached via its website (https://mchsmuseum.com).[499]

Josselyn's photographs are also part of the online collections of several museums and institutions, including:

- Monterey Museum of Art[500]
- International Center of Photography[501]
- Columbia University[502]
- Art, Design & Architecture Museum[503]
- San Francisco Maritime Museum[504]

His theater photography collections are digitally preserved and accessible through:

- California State Library[505]
- *Calisphere* (via the California Digital Library) [506]
- Harrison Memorial Library's Internet Archive.[507]

Additional collections of his work can be found at:

- Bancroft Library[508]
- Monterey County Free Libraries[509]
- Mayo Hayes O'Donnell Library[510]

ABOUT THE AUTHOR

M y name is Gregory Ford Henderson, with my middle name coming from my maternal grandfather, Byington Ford who helped develop Pebble Beach. Carmel Woods, and Carmel Valley. I was born on July 29, 1953, in Carmel, California, at 8:22 in the evening at Peninsula Community Hospital. I am the second of five children born to Alexander D. Henderson III and Patricia Ford Crass. My birth was announced in *The Monterey Peninsula Herald*.[511] [512]

From 1950 to 1957, my family lived in San Jose, California. At age 4, on July 5, 1957, we moved to Fort Lauderdale, Florida so my father could reconnect with his father, his stepmother Lucy, and his half-brother Doug.

We initially lived in a small cottage on my grandfather's property, Avon-by-the-Sea, in Pompano Beach. The apartments were located across the street from his Hillsboro Country Day School, which we attended as children. The property featured rows of individual cottages surrounding a large pool, where I loved to swim, and it offered a beautiful view of the ocean. In the summer of 1967, because of my parents' divorce, we moved back to California, so my mother could reconnect with her mother and two sisters living in the Monterey County. I started high school at Robert Louis Stevenson School in Pebble Beach and graduated in 1972. I then returned to live with my mother and stepfather in their home in Atherton, California, while going to college at Menlo College, a private institution in Menlo, California, that specialized in a two-year Associate of Arts degree in business. Most of my coursework was through the School of Business Administration, and in 1974, I graduated with an AA degree in business.

In the fall of 1974, at age 21, I transferred to the University of the Pacific (UOP) in Stockton, California, for the 1974-75 academic year. I initially moved into a one-bedroom apartment in Stockton, and at UOP, I majored in Religious Studies. In 1984, at age 34, I finally graduated from San Francisco State University (SFSU) with a BS degree in Business and Information Systems. That same year, I purchased my first computer—an Apple Macintosh—for $2,500. It had no hard drive and operated using two 3.5-inch floppy disks. What sold me on the Mac was its groundbreaking graphical user interface.

In September 1984, my first job out of college was as a programmer for Lockheed Missiles & Space (now Lockheed Martin Corporation) in Sunnyvale, where I worked from 1985 to 1986. Not long after, I saw an ad in the newspaper for contract test engineer positions at Apple Computer—my dream job! I landed the position and worked as a Quality Assurance (QA) Engineer at Apple from 1987 to 1993. Throughout my career, I have had the opportunity to work at several other companies in the Bay Area, including two startups.

On December 30, 1989, Louise Zellie Gloor and I were married at her parents' home in Mariposa, California. We had a beautiful wedding in the main living room, accompanied by a three-piece orchestra. A Presbyterian priest officiated the ceremony. Afterward, we enjoyed a buffet dinner at the house. Our honeymoon included time in Mariposa and a New Year's Eve celebration at Yosemite National Park.

Wedding for Katie P. Henderson and Amir M. Ghoreichi

Louise and I have four children: Ryan Alexander (1990), Christopher Ford (1992), Sean Murray (1994), and Leah Louise (1996).

In 1989, I launched the website HendersonFamilyTree.com, which serves as an online record of the Henderson family and several related surnames, including Ford, Boisot, Byington, Gloor, Stein, and Campbell.

I have published two other books: *Tirey Lafayette Ford* and *The Henderson Family and the California Perfume Company*. Both are available on Amazon Books.

Additionally, I have created many Wikipedia articles and contributed photos to Wikimedia Commons, a collection of photographs. Among the Wikipedia articles are entries about my grandfather, Alexander D. Henderson, Jr., who was a board member of Avon Products and Girald B. Henderson who founded two private schools—one in Colorado and one in Nevada—and my great-great-grandfather, Captain Joseph Henderson, a New York Sandy Hook pilot renowned for assisting in bringing the Statue of Liberty into New York Harbor.

Index

Notes

[1] "Born," *The Record*, September 27, 1883, National City, California, p. 3.

[2] Historic House Research," *Legacy 106*. San Diego, California. page 22.

[3] "History of San Diego, 1542-1908; an account of the rise and progress of the pioneer settlement on the Pacific coast of the United States," William E. Smythe, 1908, page 518.

[4] "Charles Lewis Josselyn," National year book, *Sons of the American Revolution*, 1889, page 193.

[5] Perkins, Thomas Allen (1917). *Addresses Delivered Before the California Society of the Sons of the American Revolution*. San Francisco, California: The Society, page 55.

[6] New England Historic Genealogical Society; Boston, Massachusetts; Vital Records of Pembroke, Massachusetts to the Year 1850

[7] *East Lake Weir 1875-2015*, Matthew A. O'Brian, 2015.

[8] "Historic House Research," *Legacy 106*. San Diego, California. page 22.

[9] "Real Estate Transactions," *The Sun*, February 28, 1883, San Diego, California, page 3.

[10] "Talbert Josselyn Obituary," *Carmel Pine Cone*, April 6, 1961, page 3.

[11] "South West Lodge F. and A. M., of National City," *The Record*, January 6, 1887, page 3.

[12] Claire Goldsmith, "Mizony Gives Copy of Early History of South West Masonic Lodge to Public Library," *National City Star-News*, September 26, 1957, page 14.

[13] "Take a tour of Victorian homes," *The Star-News*, September 12, 1998, page 27.

[14] Justus Rising, "Descendants of Aaron 3 Rising of Suffield, Ct," *Rising Family Association*, 1983.

[15] "Kicked by a Horse," *The Record*, November 28, 1889, page 2.

[16] "San Diego 25, Years Ago Today," *The San Diego Sun*, October 1, 1912, page 4.

[17] "Southern California Notes," *Los Angeles Evening Express*, December 15, 1893, page 3.

[18] "A Turn in Mines," *The San Diego Sun*, August 26, 1895, page 4.

[19] "Articles Of Incorporation," *The Sacramento Union*, February 7, 1896, page 2.

[20] *Mining and Scientific Press*, Vols. 79-80, July 1899, page 345, 581.

[21] Charles Lewis Josselyn in the U.S., General Land Office Records, 1776-2015, July 19, 1899.

[22] Mineral Survey No. 1327, Charles Lewis Josselyn, Guiding Star, Yuma County, Arizona, April 20, 1896.

[23] California, U.S., Arriving Passenger and Crew Lists, 1882-1959 for Lewis Josselyn

[24] U.S., City Directories 1822-1995 for San Diego, California.

[25] "C. L. Josselyn Returns From Trip to Death Valley Region," The San Diego Sun, San Diego, California, November 6, 1905, page 2.

[26] "Tent City Folk," The San Diego Sun, August 18, 1909, page 4.

[27] New York, U.S., Arriving Passenger and Crew Lists (including Castle Garden and Ellis Island), 1820-1957 for Louis Josselyn, January 19, 1910.

[28] U.S. Census of 1910, ED 147, Sheet 26B

[29] "Historic House Research," *Legacy 106*. San Diego, California, pages 22-23.

[30] "$120,000 Josselyn Estate to Three Sons". *Los Angeles Evening Express*. Los Angeles, California. January 22, 1917, page 1.

[31] "Former Resident Dies at Pasadena Home," *San Diego Union,* January 14, 1917.

[32] "Pine Needles," *Carmel Pine Cone*, March 15, 1917, page 4.

[33] *Los Angeles Evening Express*, Los Angeles, California, January 22, 1917, page 1.

[34] *The Los Angeles Times*, Los Angeles, California, December 13, 1917, p 14.

[35] United States Census, June 1880, for Worcester, Massachusetts.

[36] "Josselyn Brothers Serve in Two Wars," *Monterey Peninsula Herald,* February 19, 1945, page 10.

[37] "Coastal Development Permit Application," *California Coastal Commission*. Santa Cruz, California. May 25, 2001. pp. 3, 9, 11.

[38] "Death Takes Mrs. Alice Josselyn," *Monterey Peninsula Herald,* February 1, 1944, page 1.

[39] "Real Estate Transactions," *The Californian*, Salinas, California, December 26, 1919, p 6.

[40] U.S. Census of 1920, ED 15, Sheet 2B, January 7, 1920.

[41] "Carmel Draws Many From Eastbay Region," *Oakland Tribune* (Oakland, California), June 21, 1925.

[42] "Alice Josselyn Obituary," *Carmel Pine Cone*, February 4, 1935

[43] Carmel Documents and Records, Property File 010043003000, permit 197, April 1921.

[44] "Alice Josselyn Obituary," *Carmel Pine Cone*, February 4, 1935

[45] "Mrs. Alice Josselyn," *San Diego Union*, February 6, 1944.

[46] U.S., School Yearbooks, 1900-2016, Stanford University, 1908.

[47] U.S., City Directories, 1822-1995 for A. T. Josselyn, Stanford University, 1907, page 137.

[48] U.S., School Yearbooks, 1900-2016, University of California Berkeley, 1910.

[49] "Talbert Josselyn Obituary," *Carmel Pine Cone*, April 6, 1961, page 3.

[50] *Tellers of Weird Tales*, Artists & Writers in the Unique Magazine, August 1, 2011.

[51] "1910 Graduates Fare Far Afield," *Oakland Tribune*, Oakland, California, September 2, 1912, page 10.

[52] "Talbert Josselyn Obituary," *Carmel Pine Cone*, April 6, 1961, page 3.

[53] World War I Selective Service System Draft Registration Card for Talbert Josselyn, September 9, 1918.

[54] "Talbert Josselyn Obituary," *Carmel Pine Cone*, April 6, 1961, page 3.

[55] "Josselyn Brothers Serve in Two Wars," *Monterey Peninsula Herald*, February 19, 1945, page 10.

[56] "A Laugh in Every Line," *Carmel Pine Cone*, January 16, 1919, page 3.

[57] "Talbert Josselyn," *Carmel Pine Cone*, April 6, 1961, page 3.

[58] California, U.S., Marriage Records from Select Counties, 1850-1941

[59] "Thorton-Josselyn Nuptials Take Place," *Oakland Tribune*, August 6, 1927, page 5.

[60] "Tal Josselyn and Mrs. Florence Thornton Married," *Carmel Cymbal*, August 10, 1927, page 2.

[61] US Census, 1900, Santa Clara, California, Gilroy Township, June 1900.

[62] "Florence Josselyn, former Carmel councilwoman, dies," *Carmel Pine Cone*, June 4, 1992, page 9.

[63] "The Weekly Sun 1991-10-03 and Carmel-by-the-Sea 75th Anniversary Edition," *The Weekly Sun*, October 3, 1991, page 8.

[64] "Barbara Josselyn," California Birth Index, 1905-1995, January 3, 1929.

[65] Coastal Development Permit Application," *California Coastal Commission*. Santa Cruz, California. May 25, 2001. pp. 3, 9, 11.

[66] 1950 United States Federal Census, Alameda County, California.

[67] "Alameda County Marriage Licenses Issued," The San Francisco Examiner, San Francisco, California, May 24, 1957, page 51.

[68] Rachel J. Asa, California Birth Index, September 25, 1961, Alameda, California.

[69] "Talbert Josselyn," *Carmel Pine Cone*, April 6, 1961, page 3.

[70] 1940 United States Federal Census, Monterey County, California.

[71] "Florence Josselyn, former Carmel councilwoman, dies," *Carmel Pine Cone*, June 4, 1992, page 9.

[72] *Tellers of Weird Tales*, Artists & Writers in the Unique Magazine, August 1, 2011.

[73] "Monterey Patrol, by Talbert Josselyn," *Monterey Peninsula Hearld*, February 26, 1943, page 1.

[74] "Florence Josselyn, former Carmel councilwoman, dies," *Carmel Pine Cone*, June 4, 1992, page 9.

[75] "Green Valley," *The Country Guide*, Volume 72, June 1953, page 11.

[76] "Josselyn Junket," *Carmel Pine Cone*, April 5, 1956, page 5.

[77] "Talbert Josselyn Obituary," *Carmel Pine Cone*, April 6, 1961, page 3.

[78] "Talbert Josselyn, Writer, Dies," *Oakland Tribune*, Mon, Apr 3, 1961 ·Page 21

[79] "Florence Josselyn, former Carmel councilwoman, dies," *Carmel Pine Cone*, June 4, 1992, page 9.

[80] Historic House Research," *Legacy 106*. San Diego, California. page 23.

[81] "California, U.S., World War I Soldier Service Cards and Photos, 1917-1918," for Winsor Josselyn.

[82] "Winsor Josselyn Writes from the Hospital Corps Training Camp," *Carmel Pine Cone*, July 5, 1917, page 4.

[83] Howard Waldorf, "News of Flying, Fliers Picked Up Here And There," *The Oakland Post Enquirer*, Oakland, California, June 17, 1943, page 15.

[84] Pitts, Edmund M. (1922). *Base Hospital 34 in the World War*. Philadelphia: Lyon & Armor. pages 106, 248, 305, 312

[85] U.S., Historical Students Database, 1893-1946 for Winsor Josselyn, 1919.

[86] "Dry Water," *Popular Magazine*, November 7, 1928, pages 75-85.

[87] Howard Waldorf, "News of Flying, Fliers Picked Up Here And There," *The Oakland Post Enquirer*, Oakland, California, June 17, 1943, page 15.

[88] Winsor Josselyn, "Grounds Wet, No Play Let's Look' Em Over," *Carmel Pine Cone*, February 20, 1931, page 8.

[89] "People Talked About," *Carmel Pine Cone*, February 20, 1931, page 13.

[90] "Carmel Group Offers Stage Hit This Week," *The Californian*, May 17, 1933, page 8.

[91] Thompson, John. "Lewis Josselyn". *Freedom of Speech*. 4 (4), pages 8–10.

[92] Historic House Research," *Legacy 106*. San Diego, California. page 23.

[93] U.S. Patent Office, 1919, 1931, 1946, 1948

[94] Allene Fremier, "Allen Knight Beloved Eccentric," *The Boxwood Press*, Pacific Grove, 1984, p. 61.

[95] Howard Waldorf, "News of Flying, Fliers Picked Up Here And There," *The Oakland Post Enquirer*, Oakland, California, June 17, 1943, page 15.

[96] "He Flew in 1883," by Winsor Josselyn, *Harper's Magazine*, June 1940 issue, pages 28-31.

[97] "Home with Bride" *Carmel Pine Cone*, June 18, 1943.

[98] "Talbert Josselyn Obituary," *Carmel Pine Cone*, April 6, 1961, page 3.

[99] "Trudy Josselyn," 1964 Westmoor High School Yearbook, Daly City, California.

[100] Trudy A. Josselyn, San Francisco County Records Indexes, 1824-1997.

[101] "Marriages," *The San Francisco Examiner*, Oct 25, 1974, page 39.

[102] Howard Waldorf, "News of Flying, Fliers Picked Up Here And There," *The Oakland Post Enquirer*, Oakland, California, June 17, 1943, page 15.

[103] U.S. World War II Draft Registration Cards, 1942 for Winsor Josselyn

[104] "Death Takes Mrs. Alice Josselyn," *Monterey Peninsula Herald*, February 1, 1944, page 1.

[105] "Josselyn Brothers Serve in Two Wars," *Monterey Peninsula Herald*, February 19, 1945, page 10.

[106] United States Census for 1950, Alhambra, California.

[107] U.S. Sn Francisco Area Funeral Home Records, 1895-1985 for Winsor Josselyn.

[108] *Find A Grave* for Winsor Josselyn, June 14, 1973.

[109] *The Monterey County Herald*, April 3, 1961, June 15, 1973.

[110] "Eric Pape School of Art," *Boston Evening Transcript,* Boston, Massachusetts, September 10, 1902, page 8.

[111] Josselyn, Lewis (March 16, 1964). "Lewis Josselyn, Early Day Carmel Photographer, Dies", The *Monterey Peninsula Herald.* p. 2.

[112] Lewis Josselyn (1883-1964)", *Traditional Fine Arts Organization: Biographies of Carmel and Berkeley Artists.* p. 460.

[113] "Massachusetts State Building," Monterey County Historical Society, 1900.

[114] "Sweetwater Dam," Monterey County Historical Society, 1900.

[115] "Derailments At Black Butte," *www.bbcrc.org,* July 7, 1901.

[116] "Troop Train Crashes into Two Engines," *The San Francisco Call and Post.* San Francisco, California. July 8, 1901.

[117] " The Poet's Walk," *Burr McIntosh Publishing Co.* 6 (22–24). New York, N.Y.: 77 1905.

[118] Photographs are from the Monterey County Historical Society's website: *findartamerica.*

[119] U.S., Sons of the American Revolution Membership Applications, 1889-1970 for Lewis Josselyn, April 22, 1911

[120] "Honors for Popular Engaged Couple," *Los Angeles Evening Express,* February 1, 1913, page 5.

[121] Winsor Josselyn Papers 1939-1962, Inventory of John J. Montgomery Collection, *Online Archive California.*

[122] Seavey, Kent (2007). *Carmel, A History in Architecture.* Carmel-by-the-Sea, California, page 22.

[123] "Carmelites Enjoy Week-end Dance," *Monterey Daily Cypress and Monterey American,* December 8, 1914 ·Page 3.

[124] "Carmel, California," by Lewis Josselyn, *University of Nevada, Reno.* Reno, Nevada.

[125] "Pine Needles," *Carmel Pine Cone,* May 26, 1915, page 4.

[126] "1916 Calendars," *Carmel Pine Cone,* December 15, 1915, page 3.

[127] "Farwell-Surprise Party," *Carmel Pine Cone,* Jan. 5, 1916, p. 1.

[128] I. A Johnson, "Club Notes," *Carmel Pine Cone,* September 27, 1916, p. 3.

[129] "Club Notes," *Carmel Pine Cone,* January 26, 1916, page 3.

[130] " Big Wave hitting the Lone Cypress Tree on Midway Point Pebble Beach," *Monterey County Historical Society,* 1916.

[131] "Monterey Cypress," by Lewis Josselyn, *Monterey County Free Libraries.*

March 9, 1927.

[132] Julia Boynton Green, "This Enchanting Coast Verse on California Themes," *Times-Mirror Press*, 1928.

[133] "On the cover," *Carmel Valley Outlook*. Carmel Valley, California. May 29, 1975.

[134] "Pine Needles," *Carmel Pine Cone*, November 29, 1916, page 1.

[135] I. A. Johnson, "Pine Needles," *Carmel Pine Cone*, March 29, 1917, page 1.

[136] Watson, Lisa Crawford (July 6, 2015). *Legendary Locals of Carmel-by-the-Sea*. Carmel-by-the-Sea, California: Arcadia Publishing. pages 9–10.

[137] "Pine Needles," *Carmel Pine Cone*, May 10, 1917, page 3.

[138] Veterans Administration Master Index, 1917 – 1940 for Lewis Josselyn, May 21, 1917.

[139] "Gone 'Somewhere,'" Los Angeles Evening Express, Fri, Jun 15, 1917 ·Page 19.

[140] "Pine Needles," *Carmel Pine Cone*, June 28, 1917, page 4.

[141] "California, U.S., World War I Soldier Service Cards and Photos, 1917-1918," for Winsor Josselyn.

[142] U.S., Army Transport Service Arriving and Departing Passenger Lists, 1910-1939, 15 Dec 1917, Hoboken, New Jersey

[143] "Pine Needles," *Carmel Pine Cone*, January 10, 1918, page 1.

[144] Pitts, Edmund M. (1922). *Base Hospital 34 in the World War*. Philadelphia: Lyon & Armor. pp. 3, 36, 108, 147.

[145] California, U.S., World War I Soldier Service Cards and Photos, 1917-1918 for Lewis Josselyn

[146] Pitts, Edmund M. (1922). *Base Hospital 34 in the World War*. Philadelphia: Lyon & Armor. pages 106, 248, 305, 312

[147] "Josselyn Brothers Serve in Two Wars," *Monterey Peninsula Herald*, February 19, 1945, page 10.

[148] Lewis Josselyn in the U.S., Army Transport Service Arriving and Departing Passenger Lists, 1910-1939, June 23, 1919.

[149] "Brigham Young Monument Salt Lake City, Utah," Photo by Lewis Josselyn, Monterey County Historical Society, circa 1919.

[150] John Thompson, "Lewis Josselyn," *Freedom of Speech*. Volume 4, Issue 4, pages 8–10.

[151] Augustine Josselyn Obituary, *Carmel Pine Cone*, January 21, 1988, p.

20.

[152] Jean Marie Richard Marriage, France, Loire-Atlantique, Nantes, Civil Registration, 1747-1907, 14 Jan 1887, Nantes, Loire-Inférieure, France.

[153] New York City Marriage Records, 1829-1938, February 24, 1920.

[154] "It Happened in the Nutmeg State". *Carmel Pine Cone*. Carmel-by-the-Sea, California. February 26, 1920. p. 1.

[155] "Pine Needles," *Carmel Pine Cone*, March 18, 1920, page 2.

[156] "The McDuffeys Entertain At Carmel," *Oakland Tribune*, Oakland, California, March 2, 1924, page 46.

[157] New York, New York Passenger and Crew Lists, 1928.

[158] "People Talked about," *Carmel Pine Cone*, December 16, 1932, page 3.

[159] "Helene Vye's Little Shop Will Be Attractive Spot At French Fete," *Carmel Cymbal*, August 2, 1940, page 9.

[160] "Causerie Francaise Bastille Day Fete Delayed in Transit," *Carmel Pine Cone*, July 17, 1953, p. 1.

[161] Augustine Josselyn Obituary, *Carmel Pine Cone*, January 21, 1988, p. 20.

[162] Obituary for Lewis Josselyn, *Carmel Pine Cone*, March 19, 1964, page 16.

[163] California Voter Registration Index.

[164] "Coastal Development Permit Application," *California Coastal Commission*. Santa Cruz, California. May 25, 2001.

[165] "Boosts and Knocks," *Carmel Pine Cone*, February 5, 1920, p, 2.

[166] California, U.S., Voter Registrations, 1900-1968 for Winsor Josselyn.

[167] Monica Hudson, *Carmel-by-the-Sea*, Arcadia Publishing, May 24, 2006, page 23.

[168] *Monterey Daily Cypress and Monterey American*, August 5, 1922, page 2.

[169] "Art Colonists Hosts to Serra Week Pilgrims," *Oakland Tribune*, Sun, Oct 19, 1924 ·Page 54.

[170] "Dinner Party Is Held for Carmel Artists," *Oakland Tribune* Sun, Oct 04, 1925 ·Page 63.

[171] "Carmel Art Exhibition," *Carmel Pine Cone*, September 9, 1920, page 3.

[172] "Carmel's New Identity: The Peninsula's Art Colony," *The Untold History of the Carmel and Berkeley Art Colonies*. p. 187.

[173] Annual Art Exhibition Under the Auspices of the Carmel Arts and Crafts Club, August 9 to September 4, 1920

[174] "Notes". *Carmel Pine Cone*. Carmel-by-the-Sea, California. September 12, 1925. page 5.

[175] Carl Mautz, "Biographies of western photographers," Carl Mautz Publishing, 1997.

[176] "Photographers Of S.F. In Lead," *San Francisco Bulletin* Fri, Sep 04, 1925, Page 2.

[177] Irene Gaasch (April 15, 1976). "Abalone League 'a glorious league in Carmel's golden age'". *Carmel Pine Cone*. Carmel Valley, California. page 18.

[178] Frances Montgomery (May 5, 1923). "Abalone League Plays Baseball for Art's Sake". *Oakland Tribune*. Oakland, California. p. 11.

[179] Katherine Cooke, "Katrinka Swings Wicked Bat at Carmel Tourney," *Oakland Tribune*, Oakland, California, May 7, 1922, page 63.

[180] Frances Montgomery, "Abalone League Plays Baseball For Art's Sake," *Oakland Tribune*, Oakland, California, May 2, 1923, page 11.

[181] "Carmelites Return from Abroad," *Oakland Tribune*, Oakland, California, December 16, 1923, page 32.

[182] Photo of Lewis Josselyn United States Passport Applications, c. 1923.

[183] Passenger and Crew Lists of Vessels Arriving at and Departing from Ogdensburg, New York, 5/27/1948 - 11/28/1972; Microfilm Serial or NAID: T715, 1897-1957.

[184] "Carmel Fok Are Entertained by Officers," *Oakland Tribune*, Oakland, California, June 13, 1926.

[185] "U.S. Army Transport USS Mount Vernon 1917-1919," Photo by Pvt. 1 CI Lewis Josselyn, Monterey County Historical Society.

[186] "Schooner Flavel wrecked at Cypress Point," Monterey County Historical Society, December 14, 1923.

[187] "Historic Shipwreck Profile," Monterey Bay National Marine Sanctuary, December 14, 1923.

[188] "Oil Tanker Ashore At Point Pinos," *The Los Angeles Times*, May 4, 1924, page 1.

[189] "Frank H. Buck was an oil tanker," Monterey County Historical Society, May 3, 1924.

[190] "Associated Oil Company Fire," *Monterey County Free Libraries*. 1924.

[191] "USS Constitution Old Ironsides in Monterey Bay," Monterey County Historical Society, October 1, 1933.

[192] "Carmel Draws Many from Eastbay Region," *Oakland Tribune*, Oakland, California, Jun 21, 1925, Page 59.

[193] "California Tunnel Tree, Mariposa Grove, Yosemite National Park 1930, Monterey County Historical Society, 1930.

[194] "Coastal Development Permit Application," *California Coastal Commission*. Santa Cruz, California. May 25, 2001.

[195] "The Forest Theater," *Carmel Pine Cone*, December 25, 1919, page 3.

[196] "Planning Commissioner," *Carmel Pine Cone*, March 5, 1981, page 3.

[197] "National Register of Historic Places". *National Park Service*. Carmel-by-the-Sea, California. August 1988.

[198] "Coastal Development Permit Application," *California Coastal Commission*. Santa Cruz, California. May 25, 2001. pages 3, 9, 11.

[199] U.S. Census of 1930, ED 27-21, Sheet 5B.

[200] Kent L. Seavey, "Talbert Josselyn House," Lots 16, 18, Blk 82, Department of Parks and Recreation Building, Structure, and Object Record, May 3, 2002, pages 161-162

[201] Documents and Records, Santa Rita Street, Block 82, Lots 16, 18, City of Carmel-by-the-Sea, Property File 010043010000.

[202] Kent L. Seavey, DPR-523 Form, Primary Record, Talbert Josselyn House, Lot 20, block 82, April 22, 2015.

[203] 1940 United States Federal Census, Monterey County, California.

[204] Preliminary Determination of Ineligibility for the Carmel Historic Resources Inventory, June 30, 2023, City of Carmel-by-the-Sea.

[205] "Real Estate Transfers," *Carmel Sun*, July 13, 1933, page 4.

[206] DPR-523 Form, Primary Record, Asa Property, Lewis Josselyn House, Lot 21, block 81.

[207] "Home sales the week of September 12-18, 2004," *Carmel Pine Cone*, October 8, 2004, page 2B.

[208] Coastal Development Permit Application", *California Coastal Commission*. Santa Cruz, California. May 25, 2001. pp. 3, 9, 11.

[209] Hale, Sharron Lee (1980). *A Tribute to Yesterday: The History of Carmel, Carmel Valley, Big Sur, Point Lobos, Carmelite Monastery, and Los Burros*. Santa Cruz, California: Valley Publishers. pages 2, 4, 26, 49, 75–76, 80, 147.

[210] "Forest Theater Plays," Forest Theatre Society, Carmel-by-the-Sea, 1916.

[211] "Creating Carmel: The Enduring Vision," 1922, *Salt Lake City*, pages 130-131.

[212] "Carmel Comes to Jewel City For Pageant," *San Francisco Bulletin*, Aug 26, 1915 ·Page 9

[213] "Pine Needles," *Carmel Pine Cone*, March 17, 1915, page 4.

[214] "The Western Drama Society," *Carmel Pine Cone*, May 12, 1915.

[215] "A Midsummer Night's Dream," *Calisphere, University of California.* 1915.

[216] "Forest Theatre Scene Of Clever Production," *The San Francisco Examiner*, July 19, 1915, page 7.

[217] "'First Poet' is very Forceful Production," *Monterey Daily Cypress and Monterey American*. Monterey, California. July 21, 1915. p. 4.

[218] "Summer Productions," *Carmel Pine Cone*, July 14, 1915, page 1.

[219] "Man From Home Will Son be Here," *Carmel Pine Cone*. Camel, California. 4 Aug 1915, page 1.

[220] "Forest Theater Plays," Forest Theatre Society, Carmel-by-the-Sea, 1916.

[221] "Moving Picture Program for August," *Carmel Pine Cone*, August 2, 1916, page 2.

[222] "The Forest Theater," *Carmel Pine Cone*, December 25, 1919, page 3.

[223] "Tusitala To Be A Beautiful Production," *Carmel Pine Cone*, July 19, 1916, page 1.

[224] "Tusitala to be Given Here Friday Evening," *Carmel Pine Cone*, July 26, 1916, page 1.

[225] Redfern Mason (July 16, 1916)," Carmel Colony to Honor Stevenson," *The San Francisco Examiner*, San Francisco, California. page 71.

[226] "Tusitala, Stevenson Masque Scores Big Hit Before Del Monte Audience", *Monterey Daily Cypress and Monterey American*, July 22, 1916, page 4.

[227] "Pine Needles," *Carmel Pine Cone*, January 25, 1917, page 4.

[228] "Pomander Walk," by Lewis Josselyn, *California Revealed*, July 1921.

[229] "Pomander Walk Well Attended," *Carmel Pine Cone*, July 7, 1921, p. 2.

[230] "Forest Theater Opens With Pomander Walk," *The Californian*, July 5, 1921, page 8.

[231] "Caesar and Cleopatra Is in Rehearsal," The *Carmel Pine Cone*, June 8,

1922, page 1.

[232] "Ruth Kuster in the play *Caesar and Cleopatra*," *Harrison Memorial Library,* Carmel-by-the-Sea, California, July 1922

[233] "The Forest Theater, Carmel, Cal.," The Christian Science Monitor, Boston, August 2, 1922, page 10.

[234] Flecker, James Elroy (1922). *Hassan*. New York: Alfred A. Knopf.

[235] Susan Porter, "Costumes, Mechanical Detail and Makeup for Forest Theater Play," *Carmel Pine Cone*, April 14, 1923, pages 1-2.

[236] *Gilliam, Harold; Gilliam, Ann (1992). Creating Carmel: The Enduring Vision. Salt Lake City. pp. 134–136.*

[237] *"Inchling, Forest Theater Children's Phantasie, Unique". Carmel Pine Cone. Carmel-by-the-Sea, California.* August 17, 1922, page 1.

[238] "Inchling Programme," *Forest Theatre Society*. Carmel-by-the-Sea, California. August 18, 1922. pages 1–2.

[239] Gilliam, Harold; Gilliam, Ann (1992). *Creating Carmel: The Enduring Vision*. Salt Lake City, pages 134–136.

[240] "Forest Theater Plans Well Under Way". *Harrison Memorial Library*. Carmel-by-the-Sea, California, 1924.

[241] "Forest Theater to Show Mr. Bunt". *Oakland Tribune*. Oakland, California. 17 Jun 1924. page 22.

[242] "1924 Mr. Bunt Cast, Grown Up and Full of Dignity, Amused to Recall Incidents of The First Production, *Carmel Pine Cone*, June 20, 1952, page 1.

[243] "Jadwiga Noskowiak in Romeo and Juliet, *Harrison Memorial Library*, July 1927.

[244] "Romeo and Juliet This Week," *Carmel Cymbal*, July 27, 1927, page 1.

[245] "Herbert Heron Former Carmel Mayor, Dies". *The Sacramento Bee*. Sacramento, California. January 8, 1968. page 22.

[246] Arts and Crafts Club Scrapbook," 1921-1926, Harrison Memorial Library.

[247] Arts and Crafts Club Scrapbook," 1921-1926, Harrison Memorial Library.

[248] "Frankincense From Francesca," *Carmel Pine Cone*, December 16, 1922, page 4.

[249] Arts and Crafts Club Scrapbook," 1921-1926, Harrison Memorial Library.

250 "Arts and Crafts Club Scrapbook," 1921-1926, California Revealed.

251 "Arts and Crafts Club Scrapbook," 1921-1926, Harrison Memorial Library.

252 Hale, Sharron Lee (1980). *A Tribute to Yesterday: The History of Carmel, Carmel Valley, Big Sur, Point Lobos, Carmelite Monastery, and Los Burros.* Santa Cruz, California: Valley Publishers. Pages 31, 46.

253 "Hopper Heads Carmel Players," *Monterey Daily Cypress and Monterey American,* December 29, 1919 ·Page 5.

254 "Back to the Drawing Board with Artist Jo Mora," *Monterey History and Art Association.* Monterey, California. 2003, page 22.

255 "Bad Man Will Strut the Stage Tonight," *Carmel Pine Cone,* Carmel-by-the-Sea, California, January 1, 1926, page 1.

256 *The Bad Man* by Porter Emerson Brown, Arts & Crafts Theater, Carmel-by-the-Sea, California, January 15-16, 1926.

257 "Mora's Portrayal Of The Bad Man True To Living Character," *The Californian,* Salinas, California, October 25, 1928, page 3.

258 "Carmel's Beauty Theme for Blocks," *Carmel Pine Cone,* January 7, 1927, page 10.

259 Bostick, Daisy; Castelhun, Dorthea (1925). *Carmel at Work and Play.* pages 73-74.

260 Daisy F. Bostick (March 29, 1924). "Gay Carmel to Act Up in Own Theater". *San Francisco Bulletin.* San Francisco, California. p. 23.

261 "The Drama," *Dramatic Publishing Company.* Volume 15–16, 1924.

262 Seavey, Kent (2007). *Carmel, A History in Architecture.* Carmel-by-the-Sea, California, page 72.

263 Stephen Allen Reynolds, "Carmel-- its poets and peasants, by "S.A.R.","* Pine cone Press,* 1925, page 14.

264 Browne, Ellen Van Volkenburg. "Ellen Van Volkenburg and Maurice Browne papers, 1772-1983". *University of Michigan Library.*

265 Browne, Maurice (1955). *Too Late to Lament: An Autobiography.* London: Gollancz. p. 128.

266 "Theater to Carry-on Under Canvas Following Disastrous Sunday Fire," *Carmel Pine Cone,* May 24, 1935, page 1.

267 "A Repeat Performance," *Carmel Spectator,* May 26, 1949, page 1.

268 "Back Again, Intriguing history of Carmel's Golden Bough Theatre", *Alta Vista Magazine/Monterey County Herald,* August 28, 1994.

[269] Hale, Sharron Lee (1980). *A Tribute to Yesterday: The History of Carmel, Carmel Valley, Big Sur, Point Lobos, Carmelite Monastery, and Los Burros.* Santa Cruz, California: Valley Publishers, pages 31, 46.

[270] Seavey, Kent (2007). *Carmel, A History in Architecture.* Carmel-by-the-Sea, California, page 68.

[271] Helen Hilliard, "The Weaver's of Carmel," *Oakland Tribune,* Oakland, California, November 19, 1922, p. 64.

[272] Dramov, Alissandra (2022). *Past & Present Carmel-By-The-Sea.* Charleston, South Carolina: Arcadia Publishing. page 43.

[273] Seavey, Kent (2007). *Carmel, A History in Architecture.* Carmel-by-the-Sea, California: Arcadia Pub. pp. 72–74.

[274] Kent L. Seavey (January 20, 2002). "DPR 523 Form Volume II 70 Historic Resources". City of Carmel-by-the-Sea. pp. 50–52.

[275] Carmel A History in Architecture, Kent Seavey, 2007, Arcadia Publishing, page 74.

[276] Kent L. Seavey (January 20, 2002). "DPR 523 Form Volume II 70 Historic Resources". City of Carmel-by-the-Sea. pp. 50–52.

[277] "Florist Now," *San Francisco Bulletin,* May 28, 1924, page 3.

[278] "Leon Wilson papers 1871-1980," *Bancroft Library.* Berkeley, California.

[279] Seavey, Kent (2007). *Carmel, A History in Architecture.* Carmel-by-the-Sea, California: Arcadia Publications, page 76.

[280] "John Gribner as "Long John Silver in Treasure Island: Tusitala, the 1st Episode," *Harrison Memorial Library,* July 28, 1916.

[281] Monterey County Historical Society, Carmel-by-the-Sea, California, 1916.

[282] "Thomas Fisher in the Twelfth Night," *Harrison Memorial Library,* January 1923

[283] "Ethel Turner in the play The Man Who Married a Dumb Wife," *Harrison Memorial Library,* 1924.

[284] "Richard Criley in Arms and the Man," *Harrison Memorial Library,* January 1926.

[285] "Morris Wild in Arms and the Man," *Harrison Memorial Library,* January 1926.

[286] "William T. Kibbler in Romeo and Juliet, *Harrison Memorial Library,* July 1927.

²⁸⁷ Harrison Memorial Library online at:
https://archive.org/details/harrisonmemoriallibrary or at
California Revealed at: https://californiarevealed.org/

²⁸⁸ Hiller, Peter (April 20, 2021). *The Life and Times of Jo Mora: Iconic Artist of the American West*. Gibbs Smith, page 194.

²⁸⁹ "Back to the Drawing Board with Artist Jo Mora," *Monterey History and Art Association*. Monterey, California. 2003, page 4.

²⁹⁰ Murray, Mary (1998). *Jo Mora Artist and Writer*. Monterey Museum of Art. pp. 1–2, 19, 23, 26, 32.

²⁹¹ Hiller, Peter (April 20, 2021). *The Life and Times of Jo Mora: Iconic Artist of the American West*. Gibbs Smith. pp. viii, xi, 144, 146, 186, 193–196, 203, 294, 305.

²⁹² Hiller, Peter (April 20, 2021). *The Life and Times of Jo Mora: Iconic Artist of the American West*. Gibbs Smith, page 96.

²⁹³ "Back to the Drawing Board with Artist Jo Mora," *Monterey History and Art Association*. Monterey, California. 2003, page 4.

²⁹⁴ "A renaissance man," *The Californian*. Salinas, California. November 22, 2003.

²⁹⁵ "Back to the Drawing Board with Artist Jo Mora"(PDF). *Monterey History and Art Association*. LII (3). Monterey, California. 2003, page 43.

²⁹⁶ Hale, Sharron Lee (1980). *A tribute to yesterday: The history of Carmel, Carmel Valley, Big Sur, Point Lobos, Carmelite Monastery, and Los Burros*. Santa Cruz, California: Valley Publishers. pages 2, 4, 26, 49, 75–76, 80, 147.

²⁹⁷ "Opening Dale Day Carmel Woods Lots". *Carmel Pine Cone 1922-07-20*. Carmel by the sea, California. July 20, 1922. p. 5.

²⁹⁸ "Junipero Serra Works Revived In Gig Pageant," *Oakland Tribune*, Jul 22, 1922 ·Page 4

²⁹⁹ "Carmel Woods takes shape and sells well, Serra honored with statue," *Carmel Pine Cone,* September 20, 2019, pages 29-30.

³⁰⁰ "Back to the Drawing Board with Artist Jo Mora"(PDF). *Monterey History and Art Association*. LII (3). Monterey, California. 2003.

³⁰¹ Martin J. Morgado, "Junípero Serra's legacy," 1987, Pacific Grove, California, Mount Carmel, pages 87, 91, 96, 100.

³⁰² "Sarcophagus Junípero Serra Being Wrought," *Oakland Tribune,*

November 16, 1922 ·Page 14.

303 *The Californian*, Salinas, California, October 13, 1924

304 Seavey, Kent (2007). *Carmel, A History in Architecture*. Carmel-by-the-Sea, California. Page 12.

305 Hiller, Peter (April 20, 2021). *The Life and Times of Jo Mora: Iconic Artist of the American West*. Gibbs Smith. pages. viii, xi, 144, 146, 186, 193–196, 203, 294, 305.

306 Hiller, Peter (April 20, 2021). *The Life and Times of Jo Mora: Iconic Artist of the American West*. Gibbs Smith. pages. viii, xi, 144, 146, 186, 193–196, 203, 294, 305.

307 Hiller, Peter (April 20, 2021). *The Life and Times of Jo Mora: Iconic Artist of the American West*. Gibbs Smith. pages. 146.

308 "Treasure Island Art in Preview," *Oakland Tribune*. October 13, 1938, page 4.

309 Kent L. Seavey (January 20, 2002). "DPR 523 Form Volume II 70 Historic Resources". City of Carmel-by-the-Sea. pp. 12–13.

310 "Carmel's Prosaic Dairy is Art". *Santa Rosa Republican*. Santa Rosa, California. 9 Oct 1933, page 3.

311 Thompson, John. "Lewis Josselyn". *Freedom of Speech*. 4 (4): 8–10. Retrieved May 31, 2024.

312 "Robinson Jeffers Collection COL-022". *Online Archive of California*. Los Angeles, California. 1925.

313 Jeffers Studies," *The Robinson Jeffers Association*. 16 (1, 2): 1, 25. 2012.

314 "Robinson Jeffers, Carmel poet". *California Views: The Pat Hathaway Photo Collection*, page 25.

315 "The Pat Hathaway Collection Archivist collects photo treasures". *The Californian*. Salinas, California. February 28, 1981. p. 25.

316 "Robinson Jeffers," Monterey County Historical Society, 1980

317 *Robinson Jeffers Poet 1887-1987 a Centennial Exhibition*. Occidental College. 1987. p. 22. ISBN 978-1-135-58522-8.

318 Melba B. Bennett, "Robinson Jeffers and the sea," 1979.

319 Karman, James (2011). *The Collected Letters of Robinson Jeffers*. Stanford, California: Stanford University Press. pages. 468, 634. ISBN 978-0-8047-8172-5.

320 "Bechdolt Story In Current Post," *Carmel Pine Cone*, November 13, 1936, page 6.

[321] "News Notes from Carmel by The Sea," *Monterey Daily Cypress and Monterey American*, July 10, 1922, page 4.

[322] "Bechdolt Has Article in 'Post': Photos by Lewis Josselyn". *Carmel Pine Cone*. November 13, 1941. p. 1.

[323] "James Franklin Devendorf," The *Carmelite*, February 15, 1928

[324] "Carmel A History in Architecture," Kent Seavey, 2007, *Arcadia Publishing*, page 38.

[325] Robert W. Edwards, "Jennie V. Cannon: The Untold History of the Carmel and Berkeley Art Colonies," Volume 1, *East Bay Heritage Project*.

[326] William Ritschel, Bostick, Daisy F. (1925). *Carmel--At Work and Play*. Seven Arts, page 62.

[327] "August Englund," Harrison Memorial Library, Carmel-by-the-Sea, California, 1920s.

[328] "Gus Englund Of Carmel Fame Dies". *The San Francisco Examiner*. San Francisco, California. November 5, 1935.

[329] Hale, Sharron Lee (1980). *A tribute to yesterday: The history of Carmel, Carmel Valley, Big Sur, Point Lobos, Carmelite Monastery, and Los Burros*. Santa Cruz, California: Valley Publishers. pp. 27, 54, 58.

[330] "Charles King Van Riper," *Harrison Memorial Library*, 1924.

[331] Michael J. Phillips (July 9, 1924). "Remsen Play Wins Approval in Performance at Carmel". *The Morning Press*. Santa Barbara, California. p. 8.

[332] "Early California Arts at California View Archives," Pat Hathaway Collection, Monterey County Historical Society, Carmel-by-the-Sea, California, 1930.

[333] "Artist Biography & Facts Ferdinand Burgdorff". *askART*. Retrieved December 3, 2023.

[334] Alissandra Dramov, "Carmel-by-the-Sea, The Early Years," AuthorHouse, 2012, page 187

[335] Harrison Memorial Library, Carmel-by-the-Sea, California, 1915.

[336] Anne Burroughs (August 24, 1922). "*Inchling* Makes Hit at the Forest Theater". *Carmel Pine Cone*. Carmel-by-the-Sea, California. page 1.

[337] "Thomas Vincent Cator," Arts and Crafts Club Scrapbook, 1921-1926, California Revealed, 1925.

[338] "Ocean Avenue," *Carmel at Work and Play*, Daisy F. Bostick, 1925, p. 38.

[339] "Josephine Guilbert," *Flicker,* 1916

[340] "John Northern Hillard," *California Revealed,* 1916

[341] "Theodore Criley," *Point Lobos,* Monica Hudson, page 97, 1920s.

[342] "Helen MacGowan Cooke," *Harrison Memorial Library,* 1925.

[343] Sam Powers, Daisy F. Bostick, *Carmel at Work and Play,* January 1, 1925, page 91.

[344] "James Hopper," *Harrison Memorial Library,* 1925

[345] Gene Byrnes, Daisy F. Bostick, *Carmel at Work and Play,* January 1, 1925, page 95.

[346] Perry Newberry, Daisy F. Bostick, *Carmel at Work and Play,* January 1, 1925, page 95.

[347] Joseph Hand, Daisy F. Bostick, *Carmel at Work and Play,* January 1, 1925, page 91.

[348] Delos Curtis, Daisy F. Bostick, *Carmel at Work and Play,* January 1, 1925, page 91.

[349] "John Catlin," Monterey County Historical Society, Salinas, California, 1928.

[350] "Interesting Carmelites Thomas Bickle," *Carmelite,* March 7, 1928, p. 1.

[351] California Views: The Path Hathaway Photo Collection, 1929.

[352] Monica Hudson, Images of America Carmel-by-the-Sea, Arcadia Publishing, 2006, page 112.

[353] Jeff Norman, *Big Sur,* Arcadia Publishing, 2004, page 35, 80, 94, 101, 103, 116

[354] "Pine Needles," *Carmel Pine Cone,* September 30, 1920, page 1.

[355] Lussier, Tomi Kay (1979). Big Sur: a complete history & guide. *Big Sur Publications.* Page 50

[356] Paula Walling (1978). The Construction of Highway One. *The Big Sur Gazette.* Pages 14-15.

[357] "Items Of Interest," *Carmel Pine Cone,* September 18, 1919, page 2.

[358] Lussier, Tomi Kay (1979). *Big Sur: a complete history & guide,* page 43.

[359] Carmel, A History in Architecture by Kent Seavey, 2007, Arcadia Publishing, page 17.

[360] Jeff Norman, *Big Sur,* Arcadia Publishing, 2004, page 35.

[361] "Coast Highway South of Big Sur," *Monterey County Free Libraries,* 1928.

[362] Jeff Norman, *Big Sur,* Arcadia Publishing, 2004, page 100.

[363] "Finding Aid to the Save the Redwoods League photograph collection. 1885-2014," *Online Archive of California*

[364] *The Californian*, Salinas, California, March 09, 1983, page 8.

[365] Sharon Lee Hale, "A tribute to yesterday," *Valley Publishers*. 1980, page 147.

[366] Lussier, Tomi Kay (1979). *Big Sur: a complete history & guide*, page 28.

[367] John Walton (2010). "Robinson Jeffers: Historical Perspectives," *University of California Press*, Volume 87, page 28.

[368] "Big Sur Post Office and Pfeiffer's Resorts," California Views, the Pat Hathaway Photo Collection.

[369] John Walton, "The Land of Big Sur," *California History*, Volume 85, Number 1, 2007.

[370] Lussier, Tomi Kay (1979). *Big Sur: a complete history & guide*, page 44.

[371] "Sur Lighthouse," Monterey Museum of Art, Monterey, California, Gift of Jehanne B. Williamson

[372] "Remember When?". *Carmel Pine Cone*. Carmel-by-the-Sea, California. 1973-11-28. p. 4.

[373] "Carmel Beach, Carmel Point, and Point Lobos," Monterey County Historical Society, Salinas, California, 1925

[374] "The Allen House," Peninsula Diary *Mayo Hayes O'Donnell*, April 15, 1957

[375] "Allen House. First Frame House in California," *Paul C. Koeber Co.*, 1928

[376] "Monterey Pioneer Bakery," *Monterey County Historical Society*, 2024.

[377] "Carmel's real "first Murphy" family settled what U.S. Surveyors called "below Average" land," *Carmel Pine Cone*. Carmel-by-the-Sea, California. 1997-06-20. pp. 41–42.

[378] "Looking SW at the Murphy Barn," *Pat Hathaway California Views*, Monterey, California, 1919.

[379] Kent L. Seavey (July 1, 2002). "Department Of Parks and Recreation," National Park Service, pages 224-225.

[380] "Robert Louis Stevenson's Monterey Home," Oakland Tribune Oakland, California, October 15, 1922, page 25.

[381] "Adobe Tour, 1982," The Classmate: Naval Postgraduate-School Officer Students' Wives' Club Magazine, April 1983, page 35.

[382] Carmel A History in Architecture, Kent Seavey, 2007, *Arcadia*

Publishing, page 33.

[383] "Fisherman's Wharf, Monterey, California," *Monterey County Historical Society*, 2024.

[384] Monterey County Historical Society, Salinas, California.

[385] "Associated Oil Company Fire, soon after start of fire". *Monterey County Free Libraries*. Salinas, California. September 14, 1924.

[386] "Hotel Del Monte Ruins," *Monterey County Free Libraries*, 1924.

[387] "1920-30: U.S. Keeps Cool with Coolidge, *The Californian*, Jun 12, 1950, Page 42.

[388] "Hotel Del Monte, Monterey". *California Views: The Pat Hathaway Photo Collection*.

[389] Seavey, Kent (2007), "Carmel A History in Architecture," *Arcadia Publishing*, page 108.

[390] "Amelia Gates Building," Monterey County Historical Society, Pat Hathaway Collection, May 1924.

[391] Seavey, Kent (2007), "Carmel A History in Architecture," Carmel-by-the-Sea, California, *Arcadia Publishing*, page 75.

[392] "La Playa Hotel," Pictures by Lewis Josselyn in 1932, courtesy of the Monterey County Historical Society

[393] Richard N Janick (September 21, 2002). "Department Of Parks And Recreation" (PDF). National Park Service.

[394] "Mortimer Fleishhacker house, Woodside, Calif". *Columbia University Libraries*. 1925.

[395] "Highlands Inn," *Carmel at Work and Play*, Daisy F. Bostick, 1925, p. 26.

[396] Pine Inn, *Carmel at Work and Play*, Daisy F. Bostick, 1925, page 38.

[397] "D. L. James House," *Carmel at Work and Play*, Daisy F. Bostick, 1925, page 74.

[398] Anne C. Roark (22 July 1984). "Literary Alias Bared; 'Latino' Is an Anglo". *Los Angeles Times*. p. 1.

[399] "Sunset School," Monterey County Historical Society, 1926.

[400] "The History of Sunset Center". *Carmel Pine Cone*. Carmel-by-the-Sea, California. July 15, 1976.

[401] "Carmel: Its poets and peasants," by Stephen Allen Reynolds, 1927.

[402] Alissandra Dramov, "Historic Buildings of Downtown Carmel-by-the-Sea, "*Arcadia Publishing*, 2019, page 74.

[403] Kent L. Seavey (November 18, 2002). "Department Of Parks and

Recreation," pages 33-34.

[404] *Seavey, Kent (2007). Carmel, A History in Architecture. Carmel-by-the-Sea, California. pp. 99, 106.*

[405] Kent L. Seavey (January 24, 2002). "Department Of Parks and Recreation". National Park Service, pages 129-132.

[406] "El Paseo," Jo Mora Sculpture," *Kent L. Seavey (January 20, 2002). "Department Of Parks And Recreation, Primary Record."*

[407] Alissandra Dramov, "Historic Buildings of Downtown Carmel-by-the-Sea, *"Arcadia Publishing*, 2019, page 82.

[408] Richard N. Janick (May 22, 2002). "Department Of Parks And Recreation" (PDF). National Park Service.

[409] "Sally's Tea Room," Monterey County Historical Society, Salinas, California, 1928.

[410] "Municipal Rose Garden with Colton Hall in background," *Monterey County Free Libraries,* 1929.

[411] *The Bancroft Library,* "A San Francisco viewbook and photographs of historic buildings of Monterey," 1929

[412] " Colton Hall," *Monterey County Free Libraries.* 1924.

[413] "San Diego Mission in Mission Valley California," Monterey County Historical Society, 1909

[414] "The Plaza Church Los Angeles," Monterey County Historical Society, 1915

[415] "Mission San Francisco Solano Sonoma California," Monterey County Historical Society, circa 1920

[416] "San Carlos Church," *Monterey County Free Libraries.* 1929.

[417] "California Missions and Churches," Mayo Hayes O'Donnell Library

[418] John Thompson, "Lewis Josselyn," *Freedom of Speech.* 4 (4), pages 8–10.

[419] Sharon Lee Hale, "A tribute to yesterday," *Valley Publishers.* 1980, page 2.

[420] "California Missions, Towns, and Buildings: Pictorial Material from the Aubrey Drury Papers". *Bancroft Library.* Berkeley, California.

[421] Omer, Engelbert. *The last of the conquistadors, Junípero Serra, 1713-1784.* New York, Harcourt, Brace. p. 211, 1956

[422] The Pat Hathaway Collection Archivist collects photo treasures". *The Californian.* Salinas, California. February 28, 1981. p. 25.

[423] "Lewis Josselyn". *International Center of Photography.* Manhattan, New

York. December 11, 2019.

[424] Neal Hotelling (8 Nov 2019). "When Carmel rallied for those who served," *Carmel Pine Cone*. Carmel-by-the-Sea, California. pp. 26, 38.

[425] Monterey County Historical Society, Salinas, California, 1932.

[426] "SBCAA: Jarvis House (Carmel, Calif.)". *AD&A Museum UC Santa Barbara*. Carmel, California. 1920s.

[427] "National Register of Historic Places," *National Park Service*. Carmel-by-the-Sea, California. August 1988.

[428] "The Flanders Mansion Historic American Buildings Survey," *City of Carmel*. Carmel-by-the-Sea, California. March 2014. pp. 3–4, 9, 12–13.

[429] "Much Building Activity Around Carmel Now," *Carmel Pine Cone*, May 7, 1946, page 5.

[430] New Home To Be Erected For Dr. and Mrs. Brennan". *Carmel Pine Cone*. Carmel-by-the-Sea, California. 3 April 1936.

[431] Alissandra Dramov, Lynn A. Momboisse, "Historic Homes and Inns of Carmel-by-the-Sea," *Arcadia Publishing*, 2016, page 33.

[432] "Charles King Van Riper," *Harrison Memorial Library*, 1924.

[433] Paul, Linda Leigh (2000). *Cottages by the Sea, The Handmade Homes of Carmel, America's First Artist Community*. Carmel-by-the-Sea, California: Universe. p. 128.

[434] "House of the Four Winds," *Monterey County Free Libraries*

[435] Monterey County Historical Society, Salinas, California.

[436] Monterey County Historical Society, Eastside of San Antonia between 13th Avenue and Santa Lucia

[437] Monterey County Historical Society, Salinas, California.

[438] "Sherman Rose Adobe," *Monterey County Free Libraires*, 1915.

[439] "Alvarado House," *Monterey County Free Libraires*, 1916.

[440] Monterey County Historical Society, Monte Verde at 5th in Carmel, ca 1916.

[441] "Inventory," *Monterey County Historical Society*, Salinas, California, 1918.

[442] "Inventory," *Monterey County Historical Society*, Salinas, California, 1920.

[443] "Inventory," *Monterey County Historical Society*, Salinas, California, 1920.

[444] "Montgomery Block," *National Park Service*, San Francisco, California,

1920.

[445] Henry F. Dickinson House, Isabella Ave. and Scenic Dr., Monterey County Historical Society, Salinas, California, ca. 1923.

[446] Photograph available at the Monterey County Historical Society, 1925, (also known as the Hobart P. Glassel building or the Leonard Perry Building)

[447] Don Hale Sells to Barnet Segal". *Carmel Pine Cone*. Salinas, California. October 23, 1936, page 1.

[448] "A Bit of Ocean Avenue," *Carmel at Work and Play*, Daisy F. Bostick, 1925, pages 37-38.

[449] "Carmel Garage Ford show room," *Monterey County Historical Society*, 1925.

[450] Seavey, Kent (2007). *Carmel, A History in Architecture*. Carmel-by-the-Sea, California, page 68.

[451] "Fremont House," *Monterey County Free Libraries*. 1929.

[452] "Things were different then," *Carmel Valley Outlook*. Carmel Valley, California, March 20, 1975, page 13.

[453] Monterey County Historical Society, Salinas, California, 1930.

[454] "Photo Record". *Pacific Grove Museum of Natural History*. Pacific Grove, California. August 13, 1930.

[455] "Custom House," *Monterey County Free Libraries*, 1929.

[456] Monterey County Historical Society, Salinas, California, 1932.

[457] "Inventory," Monterey County Historical Society, Salinas, California, 1932.

[458] Monterey County Historical Society, Salinas, California, 1936.

[459] "Inventory," Monterey County Historical Society, Salinas, California, 1935.

[460] "Carmel Hostess Entertains at Home with Tea". *Oakland Tribune*, Oakland, California. May 2, 1926. p. 98.

[461] "Pebble Beach Homes Open For the Season," *Oakland Tribune*. Oakland, California. June 6, 1926. p. 65.

[462] The New Art Gallery at Carmel, *The Argus*, 1927, page 69.

[463] "Photographs Taken of Exhibit Of Art," *Carmel Pine Cone*, December 6, 1929, page 10.

[464] Who's Who, and Here, *Carmel Pine Cone*, December 14, 1928

[465] "Faces of a bygone era Lewis Josselyn's Pre-Depression portraits".

Carmel-by-the-Sea, California: Carmel Pine Cone. March 22, 1979. p. 11.

466 "Carmel is Coming Craft Center," *Carmel Pine Cone*, December 16, 1922, page 9.

467 Eleanor Minturn James, "North Lights," *Carmel Pine Cone*, October 9, 1931, page 8.

468 "Citizens Committee Lists Its Members," *Carmel Pine Cone,* August 31, 1934, page 1.

469 "More Requests to Keep Santa Claus Busy Climbing Down Carmel Chimneys," Carmel Pine Cone 1934-12-21, page 16.

470 "The Flanders Mansion Historic American Buildings Survey," *City of Carmel*. Carmel-by-the-Sea, California. March 2014. pp. 3–4, 9, 12–13.

471 *Carmel at Work and Play*, Daisy F. Bostick, January 1, 1925, pages 23, 26, 38, 46, 54, 62, 70, 74, 78, 86, 90, 94

472 *California Southland*, January 1927, page 2.

473 "The Village News-Reel," *Carmel Pine Cone*, June 17, 1932, page 13.

474 "The National Horticultural Magazine" (PDF). The American horticultural Society, Inc. April 1933. p. 99.

475 "The National Horticultural Magazine" (PDF). The American horticultural Society, Inc. October 1955. p. 207.

476 "In The Magazines," *Carmelite*, May 22, 1930.

477 Lester Rowntree, "Homes in the Highlands," *Sunset Magazine*, May 1930, pages 12-13.

478 *A Textbook of General Botany*, by Gilbert M. Smith, 1935

479 "Pendleton Round-Up" by Lewis Josselyn, Monterey County Historical Society, September 1929.

480 "Legion Builds Kitchen for Sunday Shoot," *Monterey Peninsula Hearld*, October 4, 1940, page 3.

481 "United States World War II Draft Registration Cards, 1942," for Lewis Josselyn, 1942.

482 "American Legion Post 512," *Carmel-By-The Sea Scrapbook*, 1935

483 Hemp, Michael Kenneth (2009). *Cannery Row: the history of John Steinbeck's old Ocean View Avenue*. Carmel-by-the-Sea, California: The History Company. pp. 24, 28, 30–32, 46, 48–49, 53, 51, 55, 69. ISBN 978-0-941425-01-8.

484 "Grove Theatre," (1936), Pacific Grove, California, Monterey County Historical Society, 1936.

[485] "A San Francisco Viewbook and Photographs of Historic Buildings of Monterey," *Bancroft Library*. Berkeley, California.

[486] "Genuine Moonlight Photography by Lewis Josselyn - Point Lobos, California," *Collectors Weekly*

[487] "Lewis Josselyn," *Carmel Pine Cone*. Carmel-by-the-Sea, California. March 19, 1964. p. 16.

[488] "Lewis Josselyn, Early Day Carmel Photographer, Dies", March 16, 1964. *The Monterey Peninsula Herald*. page 2.

[489] *Find A Grave* for Lewis Josselyn, March 14, 1964, 73981477.

[490] "Noticias del Puerto de Monterey" (PDF). *The Monterey History and Art Association*. IX (1). Monterey, California: 7. March 1965.

[491] "Old-time Carmel photos on exhibit at Sunset gallery" by Rank H. Riley, *Carmel Valley Outlook*, March 8, 1973, page 17.

[492] Elver A. Barker, "Finger painting in oils," *D. Van Nostrand Company, Inc.*, 1968, page 63.

[493] Tamara Grippi "Bring home Carmel history for Christmas," *Carmel Pine Cone*, December 14, 2001, page 44.

[494] Walter Ryce, "California Views provides Monterey County with an unparalleled trove of local photos," *Monterey County Now*, March 15, 2012.

[495] Rubén G. Mendoza. "Missions, Presidios, and Pueblos, The Hathaway Collection of Early California Photography - 1850-1990," *Boletin California Missions Foundation*.

[496] Thompson, John. "Lewis Josselyn," *Freedom of Speech*. 4 (4): 8–10.

[497] The Pacific Grove Tribune and Pebble Beach Green Sheet, Pacific Grove, California, February 28, 1973, page 3.

[498] "Two new photo exhibits are featuring this week," *Carmel Pine Cone*, March 19, 1981, page 9.

[499] ""California Views" The Pat Hathaway Collection of Historical Photographs". *Monterey County Historical Society*. Salinas, California.

[500] "Sur Lighthouse". *Monterey Museum of Art*. Monterey, California. 1935.

[501] "Lewis Josselyn". *International Center of Photography*. Manhattan, New York. December 11, 2019.

[502] "Mortimer Fleishhacker house, Woodside, Calif". *Columbia University Libraries*. 1925. OCLC 81484069.

[503] "SBCAA: Jarvis House (Carmel, Calif.)". *AD&A Museum UC Santa*

Barbara. Carmel, California. 1920s.

[504] "Museum Collections". *National Park Service.* 1920.

[505] "Discover items". *California Revealed.* 1922–1926.

[506] "Lewis Josselyn". *Clisphere-Univeristy of California.* 1915.

[507] "Lewis Josselyn". *Harrison Memorial Library.* 1922–1927.

[508] "A San Francisco Viewbook and Photographs of Historic Buildings of Monterey". *Bancroft Library.* Berkeley, California.

[509] "House of the Four Winds," Monterey County Free Libraries

[510] *Mayo Hayes O'Donnell Library.* Monterey, California.

[511] "New Citizens," Monterey Peninsula Hearld, July 29, 1953.

[512] Peninsula Community Hospital records, Carmel, California, July 29, 1953.